TOWARD SERENITY
A Common Sense Approach
To Mental Health
Based On The
Serenity Prayer

By

Vincent B. Cardarelli, Th.M., CADC

© 2003 by Vincent B. Cardarelli, Th.M., CADC.
All rights reserved.

No part of this book may be reproduced, stored in a retrieval system, or transmitted by any means, electronic, mechanical, photocopying, recording, or otherwise, without written permission from the author.

ISBN: 1-4140-1413-9 (e-book)
ISBN: 1-4140-1412-0 (Paperback)
ISBN: 1-4140-1411-2 (Dust Jacket)

Library of Congress Control Number: 2003097687

This book is printed on acid free paper.

Printed in the United States of America
Bloomington, IN

1stBooks — rev. 11/13/03

Dedication Page

For Giacobbe Cardarelli: Sapient, Balladeer, Poet

Table of Contents

Dedication Page iii

Section I—Serenity 1

    1. Toward Serenity 3
    2. The Buck Stops Here 6
    3. Life is More a Trip Than a Destination 9
    4. Yearning Rocks The Boat of Serenity 12
    5. Serenity in the Face of Strong Emotions 15
    6. Serenity and Serendipity 19
    7. Journal-izing as a Way to Insure Serenity 22
    8. The Quick Fix 25
    9. Humor and Serenity 29
   10. Elusive Serenity 33
   11. Responsibility and Serenity 35

Section II—Marriage and Relationship 39

    1. Attachment #1 41
    2. Attachment #2 44
    3. Attachment #3 47
    4. Infatuation 50
    5. Insurance Policy 53
    6. Fight Fair 57
    7. Vindication is Not The Same As Serenity 60
    8. Ventilate and Validate, Part I 63

9. Ventilate and Validate, Part II 66
10. Relationships Need To Reach For a New Level 69
11. Expectations and Marriage 72
12. Compromise and Marriage 76
13. The Fearsome Foursome #1 79
14. The Fearsome Foursome #2 82
15. Perception is "Truth" 85
16. Intimacy and Serenity #1 89
17. Intimacy and Serenity #2 92
18. Intimacy and Serenity #3 95
19. Love, Sex and Serenity 98
20. Sex Alone Does Not Sustain a Relationship 101
21. The Joys of Friendship 104

Section III—Parents and Children 107
1. Imprinting #1 109
2. Imprinting #2 112
3. Imprinting #3 115
4. The Loss of Innocence 119
5. Prolonged Adolesence 122
6. The Family #1 125
7. The Family #2 129
8. Children and Serenity 133
9. Two Diary Entries About My Stepfamily 136

Section IV—Therapy and Mental Health 139
1. Counseling is Sometimes Used to Regain Serenity 141
2. Disease or Bad Habit 144
3. Original Script 147
4. I Made A Mistake? — or — I Am A Mistake? 150
5. Complex Problems 153
6. Perfectionism, by Being Self Defeating, Prevents Serenity 156
7. Men Need a Second Chance 160
8. Men Need a Positive Self—Image to Experience Serenity 164

10. Panic Attacks A Tear in the Fabric of Serenity 171

Section V—Aging and Losses 175

1. Losses and Grief.. 177
2. Handling Losses #1 180
3. Handling Losses #2 183
4. Serenity and the September of My Years 186
5. Serenity and Senior-i-tis: 189
6. Gee, I'm Terribly Sorry, But I'm Drawing A Blank 192
7. Chronically Ill.. 195

Section VI—Alcohol and Drugs.. 199

1. Alcoholism #1 201
2. Alcoholism #2 205
3. Alcoholism #3 208
4. Co-Dependency: 211
5. Recovery From Codependency 215
6. Study on Binge Drinking Proves What We Already Know.. 218
7. Binge Drinking is Getting the Attention it Deserves. 221
8. On the Use of Medication to Attain Serenity 225

Section VII—Letting Go 229

1. Letting Go of the Past Leads to Serenitiy 231
2. Letting Go #2.. 234
3. Letting Go #3.. 238

Section VIII—Spirituality and Faith 241

1. On The Need For Faith In Our Quest For Serenity 243
2. 'Owned Faith' Gives Answers to Life Questions ... 247
3. False Pride 251
4. The Spirituality Of Imperfection 254
5. Ah! Sweet Mystery of Life 257
6. Discernment.. 260

7. Sic Transit Gloria Mundi 263
8. Forgiveness 266
9. Cutting Corners on Honesty 269
10. "Carpe diem" Philosophy Reduces Anxiety 272

Section IX—The Thirteenth Step 275
1. The Thirteenth Step: Surrender of the Ego: 277

Appendix: 281

About the Author 283

Section I—Serenity

1. TOWARD SERENITY

It's a Journey Toward a Goal

*God grant me the Serenity
To accept the things I cannot change,
The courage to change the things I can
And the wisdom to know the difference.*

The Serenity Prayer, as it is known, sets the theme for a series of articles I wrote that appeared over several years under the title *Toward Serenity*. The entire prayer, printed in full below, is attributed to Reinhold Neibuhr, a Protestant theologian.

I believe that no one ever really reaches total serenity. *Working toward serenity*, however, which is the point of this book, grants the seeker enough peace of soul to travel the journey of life to make it worthwhile.

Serenity is the ultimate goal of each person's effort to be happy; it is the state of soul described as imperturbable, calmly being at home with the world and with one another.

And so, even though one never "arrives" at the goal, imagine the amount of distance that one covers in the attempt.

The title includes the word "toward" because it implies a motion and direction. The self—or soul—strives for

Vincent B. Cardarelli, Th.M., CADC

serenity, and although it is a goal, we must realize that one never captures it wholly or constantly, but that sometimes we will lose serenity and be tempted or agitated. It is the effort *toward* - the journey—that gradually provides what we are looking for.

Serenity is not a quick fix. Alcohol or drugs, prescribed or not, give real relief. That kind of relief, however, is temporary. Some people still act like three-year-olds, in the sense that they "want what they want, and they want it right away." Sometimes serendipity provides serenity, such as when one wins the lottery, or lucks out in some competition (like a Super Bowl). But normally, chance or luck do not produce serenity.

Serenity is not an impulsive decision: to spend, to eat compulsively, to knee-jerk react to a strong emotion (like anger)—these do not lead to serenity. Serenity and impulsivity are mutually exclusive.

Serenity is not an accumulation of power or wealth, which certainly satisfy narcissistic needs, but as the saying goes, they "don't buy happiness."

Serenity is not a passive, myopic prayerful "God, please take care of me." As some of the chapters will show, serenity is not giving up and giving in, nor an avoidance of responsibility.

If serenity is NOT any of those, then what is it? Serenity is the result of our own efforts. It is taking responsibility for oneself, and for one's life. In times past, we used to call it 'growing up,' or being mature.

Serenity is recognizing our emotions but not being at the mercy of them. A serene person is indeed aware of his or her feelings, but is able to use them wisely (at least most of the time.) To be guided only by feelings (remember the 70's—"let it all hang out?") IS to live a roller-coaster life, which is the opposite of serenity.

I will attempt a definition: *Serenity is the affirmation that you are a child of the universe, and that you belong here and are worthwhile. It is the conviction and feeling that, even though much of what goes on around you is vexing and dangerous, there is nevertheless a plan and you fit into it in some way, and that as long as you hang in there, it will make sense in the end. I'm not totally O.K., but that's O.K.*

The following chapter will deal mostly with mental health issues, as they bear on our emotions and the way we handle them. They will seek to empower you with strategies for coping with the stress of modern living. They don't focus so much on the "why" of your behavior, as on the "what"— what can we do about how we feel, and what is happening. Hopefully, they will help you grow "toward serenity."

Here's the entire "Serenity Prayer." It is the basis for all the ideas expressed in this book. Over the course of 50 years in the helping profession, I'm sure that I have made my own ideas and strategies that I picked up here and there. Where possible, I have given credit to the authors and sources of ideas culled from others.

> God grant me the serenity
> To accept the things I cannot change,
> The courage to change the things I can
> And the wisdom to know the difference.
>
> Living one day at a time
> Enjoying one moment at a time;
> Accepting hardship as the
> Pathway to peace.
>
> Taking, as He did, this sinful world as it is,
> Not as I would have it.
> Trusting that He will make all things right
> If I surrender to His will;
>
> That I may be reasonably happy in this life,
> And supremely happy with Him forever in the next.
> By Reinhold Neibuhr

2. THE BUCK STOPS HERE

Don't Blame Mom and Dad for Your Misfortune

I think it is time to stop the tide—one might say the crusade—against parents. There is a strong tendency to blame parents for all the ills that happen to adolescents and adult children who are in their mid-life crises.

All of a sudden, it seems we have become aware that the rise in suicides, the addictions, failed marriages, panic disorders and personal inadequacies can all be attributed to some failure of our parents in their imperfect method of raising us through the perils of childhood.

One author calls blaming parents "big business" for the helping professions.

If it isn't one thing it is another. Adult Children of Alcoholics (ACOA) are the way they are, with a page-long laundry list of personality traits, because one or both of their parents are alcoholics.

"Adult Children," it is inferred, who have been abused sexually, physically or emotionally, are not responsible for their adult behavior because of the sins of their parents. Parents who are too strict, parents who are too lax, parents who are "dysfunctional" (the latest "in" word)—all these are to blame for how a person turns out in adult life.

Often enough, having parents like that "absolves" the adult child from taking responsibility for his own actions.

Yes, it is true that one's past helps in understanding what one is going through in the present. And yes, it is true that the past is a contributing factor in the unhealthy habits that were learned in growing up.

But many of the helping people and organizations who invite adult children to recover, also cause them to be stuck in the past. They continually resurrect "what it was like," retelling their stories, and implying that if only their parents would accept the responsibility (read: Blame) for how the children turned out, then somehow that would make it easier for the children to recover from the wounds of the past, and be happier and healthier as a result.

The past helps in understanding our present selves, but it does not help in resolving the present.

In fact, often the parents themselves were victims of a hard childhood. But the generations of the past (and I am old enough to remember several generations) did not use the excuse that they acted the way they did because of their parents.

When I failed a course in school, got caught by the principal or the police, no one looked to blame my parents.

I am not advocating a return to the "good old days," but I think the pendulum has swung to the other end of the spectrum and we now see an effort to evade responsibility. One of the areas in which evasion of responsibility is most glaring is in marriages and relationships.

Judith Viorst says: "impossible expectations and unmet needs are continuing sources of marital tension and strife." In other words, each spouse expects the other to change, to meet one's unfulfilled needs and to provide the happiness that one cannot provide for oneself. She has written a book on the topic: *Grown Up Marriage.*

Often when adults go to therapy, it is a natural pitfall to focus on the past and unwittingly place blame on the past, thereby finding an excuse for recent behavior.

Vincent B. Cardarelli, Th.M., CADC

If I am not responsible for the past, it is easy to conclude that I am not responsible for the present. All therapy begins with confronting one's own baggage.

But it doesn't end there. We can look to others to understand how we got here, but managing our present and our future requires the courage to look at ourselves for the solution. To be stuck in trying to understand "why," is called "Analysis Paralysis".

Erikson said that we will have to accept that "one's life is one's own responsibility." Harry Truman said "the buck stops here."

What are the children of today's adult children going to say when they grow up? Will they blame you? When does the cycle stop? Or do we go all the way back to Adam and Eve? Serenity is the goal of an enjoyable life; responsibility is the means toward serenity.

3. LIFE IS MORE A TRIP THAN A DESTINATION

In my family, we were always doing for others. My father came to America to make money so that he could send it back to his family. He gave them the potential to step up from poverty and eventually move into the middle class in Italian society. My mother, also an immigrant, sacrificed for her five younger siblings in her early years in a new country. Then she continued to do the same for her own children. Always "available."

In a sense, I have continued the pattern by working for 50 years in a helping profession, first as a priest and then as a mental health and addictions counselor. My rationale was: there'll be time for me to satisfy my own needs when I retire. I now realize that I have postponed a lot of things waiting for my train to come in.

Don't jump to conclusions thinking that I am going to say that the alternative is "to get while the getting is good." Or "God helps those who help themselves." Or even that I feel that I have squandered my life. "Me first" is not a solution nor an effective way to serenity. Rather the way to serenity is to stop and smell the roses. It is like a half-way measure between a co-dependent "I'll do for others," and a selfish "I come first."

. I was pondering this thought and sharing it with a client when, as chance would have it, the following story fell

Vincent B. Cardarelli, Th.M., CADC

out of one of the books that I was donating to the library sale. I had copied it out of a book years before and now I'd like to share it with you.

It's called *The Station* by Robert J. Hastings:

> *Tucked away in our subconscious is an idyllic vision. We see ourselves on a long trip that spans the continent. We are traveling by train. Out the windows, we drink in the passing scene of cars on nearby highways, of children waving at a crossing, of cattle grazing on a distant hillside, of smoke pouring from a power plant, of row upon row of corn and wheat, of flatlands and valleys, of mountains and rolling hillsides, of city skylines and village halls. But uppermost in our minds is the final destination. Bands will be playing and flags waving. Once we get there our dreams will come true, and the pieces of our lives will fit together like a jigsaw puzzle. How restlessly we pace the aisles, damning the minutes for loitering—waiting, waiting, waiting for the station.*
>
> *When we reach the station, that will be it! We cry.*
> *When I'm 18.*
> *When I buy a new 450L Mercedes-Benz.*
> *When I put the last kid through college.*
> *When I have paid off the mortgage.*
> *When I get a promotion.*
> *When I reach the age of retirement, I shall live happily ever after.*

Sooner of later, we must realize there is no station, no one place to arrive at once and for all. The true joy of life is the trip. The station is only a dream. It constantly outdistances us.

"Relish the moment" is a good motto, especially when coupled with Psalm 11, 8:24—"This is the day which the Lord hath made: we will rejoice and be glad in it."

It isn't the heaven that we look forward to in the next world that makes us happy today; it is the heaven that we are in right now that gives serenity. It isn't the burdens of today that drive men mad; it is the regrets over yesterday and the fear of tomorrow. Regret and fear are twin thieves who rob us of today.

So stop pacing the aisles, and counting the miles. Instead, climb more mountains, eat more ice cream, go barefoot more often, swim more rivers, watch more sunsets, laugh more, cry less. Life must be lived as we go along. The station will come soon enough.

4. YEARNING ROCKS THE BOAT OF SERENITY

We just acquired a little puppy, a Bichon-Poo. It is fluffy, playful and affectionate. But as soon as I disappear from his sight, he begins to cry with a high-pitched wail. It is a whine that represents the feeling of yearning: a reaction that seems instinctual and very appropriate. He is yearning for something that is not there.

Humans, too, are often ambushed by yearning. W.B.Spencer wrote: *It is God who buried desire and aspiration so deep in the human heart.*

We have all experienced that yearning for something or someone that we cannot (or may not) have. It is a searching feeling, a pull that can only be satisfied (it seems) by what is missing.

To yearn is to desire, to aspire for something not yet possessed. It is asking for more out of life; it is the stuff of dreams. Yearning is part of the experience of losing something or someone.

Yearning is different from the competitive drive, which means to strive toward a goal.

An inner drive strengthens you, while yearning weakens you.

Without the aggressive drive, there would be no new inventions, no creative spirit that produces art and architecture, music and theatre. And yet there is only a thin line between the desire of reaching a goal, and the yearning that ambushes you.

So how do you handle it? How do you bring it under some kind of control, and free up the energy to focus on other things. You try all the old clichés, like "The grass is always greener..." Or "Be happy with what you've got." Or you may look for help elsewhere.

Self-help programs tell me that "acceptance" is the answer. That is, to let go of the desire or the yearning, and accept what is. But as soon as you relax your grip or let down your guard, there it is again. You want what you cannot have—envy and jealousy raise their ugly heads.

Religion, and spiritual gurus, have traditionally had the answer to this human riddle. G.K. Chesterton calls it "the hound of heaven," meaning that the yearning will only be satisfied when it is filled with God, and He chases you until you give in. Buddhism teaches that only Nirvana, the state of blessedness, will extinguish that search.

I think that is one of the major purposes of religion, namely, to give meaning to the desires that seem unquenchable by simply human means.

But no matter whether you use self-help or religion, whether you believe in a Higher Power, or in the Power of Humanism (or Nature), you do have to strike a happy medium between striving for what you yearn, and accepting what you cannot have.

If you stay mired in the stuff of desire, you prevent opportunities for new and different things to happen. So, for example, if you fuel the yearning for a relationship that you cannot have, and hold on to the fantasy of what cannot be, you prevent anyone else from moving into the space of your love.

W.B. Spencer, who wrote <u>Irrational Fears</u>, says that it is not fair that so many things could assail your heart and senses and ambush you along the way. Nice things: like sunlight on the waters, or the perfume of an attractive woman, or a painting that you unexpectedly see in a gallery.

Vincent B. Cardarelli, Th.M., CADC

Or ugly things: like someone offering you a drink when you are trying to abstain, or a quick fix in the time of yearning, or the temptation of a climactic moment (either in the game of lottery or of love.)

It's true, you know, it doesn't seem fair that we have such powerful desires and yearnings which seriously upset our serenity. But time has a way of dimming the unfairness of our lives.

The older we get the more we forget the disappointments of the past. Maybe forgetfulness is a good thing after all. We eventually forget what we wanted, and what we have never attained, and begin to get the "wisdom" of the elderly. As a result we grow more mellow, and more accepting of what is. We look in the mirror and finally see the crow's feet, and confess to our real age.

But in the meantime, we keep asking "why?" - Why did God put this yearning in our hearts? Is there supposed to be some kind of hidden meaning in it, since it is so universal?

But maybe the answer is simply "That's the way it is." That's Human Nature. Or maybe the answer is that if we got everything that we wanted, we would become insufferable; we would become gods unto ourselves. Wouldn't it be wonderful if we could orchestrate things to fit our plan for the world!

We become more humble with the knowledge that we are human and just like everyone else. I don't think that the purpose of unfulfilled yearnings is to humiliate us. I think it is more to keep us from getting too big for our britches.

And, you know, that last thought may just lead to another topic on how alike we all are.

Stay tuned!

5. SERENITY IN THE FACE OF STRONG EMOTIONS

It's always uncomfortable to be in the presence of strong emotions, and there are many times when you are in such a place. For example, when you need to tell someone some bad news, you hesitate because you know that you will have to deal with strong emotions coming back at you.

Another example is when you visit a relative or friend after a death. It is daunting to walk in and have to find something to say that is relevant and empathetic. You stammer, and say "Uh..." until you are able to get over the first few minutes.

It is the same in your family when, as a parent, you have to deny a request of your teen-ager, and just know that there will be an emotional reaction—usually a strong one—in response to your denial.

But the most difficult situation, and the one that sorely jeopardizes serenity, is when strong emotions erupt between spouses or lovers. Whether it is a misunderstanding, or discovering a lie, or making a hurtful statement, or whatever...these situations trigger strong emotions, like anger, disappointment, retaliation, etc. In other words, this is really a tough one.

Vincent B. Cardarelli, Th.M., CADC

And THEN...the "normal" reaction is usually strong emotions in response. And that leads to an argument. This in turn leads to the snowball effect. Pretty soon a couple is dredging up past hurts that were never resolved, and you have an impossible situation. Neither one intended for it to get this far, but there you have it anyway.

So what do you do about it? Do you walk away? Do you jump in and get your licks in? Do you interrupt when your spouse says something "wrong"? Do you let the other person "get away" with saying something that is obviously exaggerated? How is it possible to resolve anything when such powerful emotions are being hurled across the divide?

Well, it's no surprise to say that if you keep doing what you have been doing, nothing will change. The adage "you have to communicate better" is a half-truth if one believes that means to stay there and talk more, or more often. It's better to say that "you have to communicate *in a different way.*"

There is only one way for strong emotions to be resolved, and that is for them to be expressed. Sometimes, just expressing them is enough; but other times it is not.

So I think the first "new" technique that I would suggest is that when you are in the face of strong emotions, PAUSE. Just stop. Stop and listen. Don't react right away. Don't feel pressured to respond immediately. Throw yourself into neutral. Disengage your clutch—the connection between your own emotions and your tongue.

Sometimes it would be well to wait until the next day, then bring it up with an introduction, like: "You know, dear, yesterday when you were saying...Well, I've thought about it and this is what I would like to say in response..."

You might find that your spouse will surprise you by saying, "It's not a big deal anymore; I just felt better saying it to you, and the fact that you listened was enough."

Or if it was a big deal, the fact that you waited gives you perspective enough to answer with less emotion, and with a more measured and controlled response.

Strong emotions will usually trigger a strong emotional response. It's part of the fight/flight survival instinct ingrained in our genes. But as human beings we can train ourselves to overcome our "natural" instincts—those that we share in common with our animal ancestors—and act more "rational."

And in fact if we want to have "long-term relationships" that is exactly what we need to do—namely, train ourselves to act differently from what comes naturally. "Well, that's just the way I am" is not a reason, it is an excuse.

"I always tell the truth, no matter what." Yes, I know that! But you don't always have to "tell" it immediately. If only you can wait until a later time, preferably tomorrow, you may decide that you don't HAVE to tell it at all.

Sometimes, the nature of the topic is such that you do have to keep the communication going right now. Well, then a mini-version of "waiting" or 'not-reacting" immediately is to follow the rule: Don't interrupt. Wait until the strong emotion spends itself. And then ask for enough time to say what you need to say without your spouse interrupting.

Walking away from strong emotions does not resolve difficult situations. Jumping right in and fighting it out with equal fire-power doesn't work either, since it only escalates the intensity.

Learning to control the fight or flight response at least temporarily by not reacting, or by staying emotionally neutral, sets the stage for resolving the situation.

Being in charge of your own emotions works more often than not. When you walk up to a grieving person, you don't immediately have to come up with something clever or soothing. You can just be calm and quiet, and often enough that is satisfactory.

In the same fashion, in an emotionally-charged situation with your spouse, you don't have to come up with a defensive barrage immediately. You can learn to wait until the air clears, and you, in turn, will have your say.

To be honest, I'm not so sure that it will work as well with a teen-ager who knows how to be insistent enough to make you either want to run or yell back: "That's enough."

But I do believe that if your teens know that you WILL get back to them in a timely fashion, they will learn to accept your style.

Confronting strong emotions with strong emotions is called an argument. On a larger scale, confronting strong emotions with strong emotions is war—gang war, or war between nations. So the two "new" rules of handling strong emotions are: 1) Pause long enough to be in charge of your own emotions; and 2) Don't interrupt. Don't let your "fight- or- flight" instant response hi-jack your brain. Serenity depends on keeping the safety on our emotional trigger (as well as on the trigger of hand-guns.)

6. SERENITY AND SERENDIPITY

Serenity Depends on Discipline, not on Serendipity

I recently tuned in to a TV talk show in which a "bad guy" movie star was recounting how he had a spiritual conversion. As a result of it, he gave up his addiction to drugs and alcohol and committed himself to the Lord. He ended his story by saying, "I put the discipline of Christianity into my life."

Please read on: this is not a sermon.

The bad guy had learned the hard way what many people already know; that a happy life is not the result of serendipity, it is the result of discipline and diligence.

Serendipity is a fortunate experience that happens by accident. It makes you happy, but you can't count on it.

Discipline is a training, or a set of rules, that produces a specific pattern of behavior. The purpose of discipline is to help people live life in a peaceful, orderly and happy way. And to live in harmony with others.

The word "discipline," can have other meanings, like punishment or military life. But here it means a way of life as taught by parents, or a group to which one belongs.

The primary examples are the major religions, or other groups like A.A., Yoga, therapy groups, support groups, etc. Each one teaches its own version of discipline, and when its members follow the rules, the promised result is received.

You can carry discipline to an extreme, as when you are racked with guilt because you said or did something wrong and can't forgive yourself (obsessive-compulsive); or when you demand 100 percent obedience from your children or members of your family and can't forgive them for a mistake (rigidity.) That is what is meant by the adage: Keeping the letter of the law instead of the spirit of the law.

Without discipline in one's life, you will be tempted to live a life of impulse. And then, impulsivity can grow into an addiction—to alcohol, gambling, shopping, drugs, physical and/or verbal violence. "I can't help myself" is usually the rationalization.

So what can we conclude from all that?

Well, first of all, that the word "discipline" is not so bad. There's a Latin proverb—*in medio virtus stat*—which, applied here, means that discipline is a happy medium between the two extremes of rigidity and impulsivity.

The value of discipline is that it gives orderliness to one's thinking and behavior.

Religion, A.A., and other guidance programs help in the sense that the structure is laid out for you; it tells you what to do and what to avoid. As a result, you live life down the middle of the road—a balanced approach to life—and you don't have to recreate the wheel by figuring it out by yourself. You simply follow the rules.

The ideal, of course, is to internalize the discipline so it will become one's own and not just a robot-like performance of duty. Thus, like the converted movie star, one will be "saved" or sober or serene; i.e., one will attain the goal. Not by luck, or serendipity, but as a result of "the program." "Follow me," says the teaching, "and you will have the prize."

There are, in our nation, over 200 "ways"—religions, self-help groups, Eastern philosophies, etc. Each one, in my opinion, if adhered to, will produce a satisfied life. I don't believe that any one is better than another, although some of them claim exclusivity.

Briefly then, the quest for serenity begins when a set of rules is given to you in infancy, through early childhood and into adolescence. When we mature, hopefully we have made the rules and training a part of our habitual life so we don't have to think about it every time we are faced with a decision. Against this "regular"- some say boring—lifestyle, we can then fit in spontaneity and serendipity for the highs of life. We don't have to manufacture the highs of life artificially with drugs or alcohol. Happiness is made, it is not found.

We then welcome the highs of serendipity—what happens by chance—because like the cream on the cake, it adds to what we already have, but in and of itself, it does not produce serenity.

7. JOURNAL-IZING AS A WAY TO INSURE SERENITY

This book grew out of a series of articles on Serenity that I wrote for a newspaper. It was a challenge to write about the topic, and not use myself and my experiences as the criteria. It tends to become personal, whether I want that or not. A therapist, I learned, needs to keep himself from getting involved. But it's no secret to you that from time to time I have had to struggle to maintain a sense of balance while surrounded by sadness, trauma and anxiety.

One of the ways that has been of great help to me is to keep a Journal. *journalizing.*

A journal is not the same as a diary. A diary logs events and encounters and things that you don't want to forget.

A journal, on the other hand, keeps a record of your feelings, your reactions to the events that occur in your life. It's like your "sponsor," your conscience, your "Jiminy Cricket."

Looking back on your thoughts and feelings as your life unfolds begins to throw light on the real you, on your reactions, on the secret you that mostly no one knows. And sometimes you don't even know yourself. Reading over your notes and *re-experiencing yourself,* becomes a lesson that you teach yourself.

When you have been keeping the journal for a number of years, you will be surprised—pleasantly or unpleasantly - at the fact that you were here before. What you are experiencing is not new; it's *deja' vu.* You can be happy with that revelation, or you can be chagrined.

But either way you will be able to decide what you want to do about it, without having the shame of someone "giving you feedback." You may even read one of your notes that said "Darn, I don't want to learn that lesson again." And here you are, indeed, learning the same lesson again.

Another advantage of keeping a journal, is that you will become acutely aware of the imperfection of life, *your* life. You aim at perfection, and your *human-ness* hits you smack-dab in the face. Humiliating? At first it is, but then you become more accepting of yourself with your limitations and warts. And maybe you will extend that acceptance to others as well, especially members of your family.

Another benefit of journalizing is that you can practice beforehand for some confrontation, or important communication that looms ahead.

If it's with the boss, you can write your script (which may not come out exactly the way you practiced it), and then be less prone to say something stupid or self-effacing.

If it's with one of your loved ones, you'll be able to critique what you want to say before you put your foot in your mouth. So before you say "You're a slob," you may be able to prepare, be in control and say: "When you leave things lying around, I am prompted to pick up after you, and then I feel like a servant rather than your spouse."

Sure, it's a confrontation, but it's more likely to lead to change than an insult.

You know, when we are with friends and acquaintances, we naturally monitor our words and feelings, so that we will not intentionally hurt the other. "Familiarity breeds contempt" is the old saying that reminds us that we drop our guard with those we know and act impulsively

Vincent B. Cardarelli, Th.M., CADC

rather than thoughtfully. The Journal is a way of keeping us on our toes.

Reading over the Journal also helps you to evaluate your reactions. For example, from a distance you may realize that you over-reacted to something. That will be a self-taught lesson that says "Don't sweat the small things." Therapists make a lot of money teaching people on how to avoid stress by not making mountains out of mole-hills.

Another benefit- you will have a written record of your successes and emotional highs. My wedding, my bonus, my child's first date, the particulars of my memorable vacation—verbal pictures that do not fade. You don't get a Silver Star for any of these events, but you will recapture the feelings and satisfaction of the past, all of which make up what you are now.

The Journal is an accurate picture of your courage in the face of adversity, or your humility in the face of success, and a conviction that says: "Way to go. You made it!"

Some people use therapy for this purpose; namely, to be reassured about life and their ability to cope with it. For some, the Journal gives the same result. It provides the realization that your life has its ups and downs and that you are able to cope with whatever helps you to maintain your serenity, or to restore it when it is jeopardized.

8. THE QUICK FIX

Rather: Take a Long-Range View

We are a nation of seekers of the quick-fix. We are *doers, take charge guys, assertive, buy now and pay later.* If there's a problem, let's fix it now. Oftentimes, however, there is no quick fix, no short-range solution to what we have to do. We need to take a long-range view in order to handle the event adequately.

Life is like a 16mm film, with a beginning and an end. In between, there are innumerable frames, representing a moment or a day in the span of that life. When you get to the end of the film, you're able to look back on the whole story, and get the big picture. From that point of view, any one frame—or incident—along the way becomes less important than the whole. You can also see how the incident fits into the whole picture.

Yet if we stop the film anywhere along the way and focus on just one frame, we may very easily get the wrong impression about the where the story was going. One frame may represent success; or one frame may represent a tragedy.

If we were able to see into the future, we could take a deep breath and wait for things to work themselves out. It is easier to sit on a plateau and look back over the path we

Vincent B. Cardarelli, Th.M., CADC

have already taken. But life is not like the old TV program *Early Edition*; we can't forestall events and make them work out the way we want—at least not always.

To take a long-range view is easy enough when the film is over. To take a long-range view halfway through the film is difficult. In the same way, we can judge the success of the film after viewing the whole of it. But we cannot predict the outcome from viewing just one of the frames.

So it is with life. We can see what it all meant when looking back. (That is usually the topic of a eulogy.) But to predict the whole of our lives by viewing just one frame is hazardous and often incorrect.

Having a long-range view may mean that you are only beginning to solve the problem. For example, a parent sees a low mark on his child's report card and reacts as if this will mean total failure. That's called "catastrophying," like Chicken Little's "The sky is falling." That's reacting to the moment—looking for the quick-fix. But you can't just ignore it, either.

I ran into a friend of mine whose child had a terrible bicycle accident about 15 years earlier. At the time, it looked like he would die. She refused to give up, even when the doctors and all around her told her it was hopeless. I asked her how he was and she said he was great, healthy and successful in his job.

George Will, a columnist with whom I often disagree, reported that "promiscuous drugging of children" for ADHD, attention deficit hyperactive disorder. He says "pharmacology is employed to relieve burdensome aspects of temperament." In other words, medicine is often given to children in hopes of a quick-fix.

It is much harder to take a long-range view, which would mean trying new discipline techniques, or classroom management to "help" the children. It's easier to "blame" an illness for the behavior of a child and then medicate. That absolves everyone from the hardship of finding a solution.

TOWARD SERENITY

"This too shall pass," is a slogan that 12-Step members tell themselves when they are faced with what looks like a tough situation, but in reality is transient. The urge is to fix it right away through alcohol, food or drugs. It would be easier if we could project ourselves down the road and be able to look back and see how it all would have turned out. "This too shall pass" is a reminder that we can't do that.

Taking a long-range view helps to cope with the impulsivity of the moment; it helps to curb the urge to seek a quick-fix.

A romantic break-up often causes panic and the urge to fill the emptiness as quickly as possible. To have a weekend without anything to do, and be all alone is painful. A phone call, an invitation...even a call to the old boyfriend...anything to relieve the distress of the moment.

You may have heard about the "The Marshmallow Study" a research project that experimented with postponing gratification. Social scientists took a group of 3-year old children and put them in a room with an adult. The adult gave them all one marshmallow and told them that he had to leave the room for a while, but when he came back, he would give another one to the children who still had the original one. Some of the children ate the marshmallow immediately after the adult left the room (instant gratification). Others were able to hold on to theirs, and received another one when the adult returned, (able to postpone gratification.)

It's not only 3-year olds who have a hard time waiting for gratification; there are many adults who find it just as difficult to take a long-range view. The study predicted which style the children would take in adulthood.

We live in an age in which instant gratification infuses all our expectations. But experience as well as research shows that impulsive urges do not make for happiness or serenity. The urge for the quick fix makes for anxiety and impatience.

Members of AA, or any 12-Step program, all of whom have been afflicted with impulsive and compulsive desires,

Vincent B. Cardarelli, Th.M., CADC

have learned that "Easy does it" and "One thing at a time, one day at a time" make for a more serene unfolding of the "frames" of our lives.

Learn to take a long-range view in handling the unpleasant and unexpected events in your life. It makes for less angst, and more serenity.

9. HUMOR AND SERENITY

Laughing is better than swallowing a pill

The ability to laugh has important implications for health, social skills and intimate relationships. Humor and serenity are closely tied together.

Every public speaker knows how to begin his speech with some humor; its purpose is to break the ice and reduce the speaker's tension. Most people will start with a joke or by poking fun at themselves.

When Al Gore ran for President, he got up and said "How do you tell Al Gore from a room full of secret service agents? He's the stiff one." He not only reduced the tension, but also beat to the punch those who would poke fun at him.

Someone with a sense of humor is a welcome addition to any party or family gathering. Oh, yeah! I like Uncle Vinnie, he makes us laugh.

But besides the social skills that laughter provides, studies have shown that laughter is good for mental and physical health. As quoted in *lifescape.com*, a good laugh:

- Relaxes muscles
- Helps breathing
- Stimulates endorphins
- Heightens energy

- Reduces tension
- Alleviates depression
- Boosts your immune system

It's like a prescription drug that we don't have to pay for. It's estimated that as children we laughed several hundred times a day, but as adults, we laugh maybe a dozen times. You don't have to go around being silly all the time, but smiling seems to be just as beneficial as a belly laugh. So it's important to develop an attitude which sees humor in one's life.

You've heard it said: "He's got on attitude." Usually that means a person is dour, a sad sack, or maybe belligerent or angry looking.

Look at yourself in the mirror and see the difference in your "normal" face and your face when you are smiling. Even forcing a smile has beneficial results.

Then there are those who take themselves too seriously. Everything is weighty: you can't joke with them too much. I have a friend to whom I purposely tell jokes, so I can see whether he "gets" them or not. Usually he doesn't. That's when I laugh at my own jokes.

Some people are defensive. Anything you say about them, they perceive as a criticism. They are so thin-skinned that they tolerate no negative feedback. Such people have a tenuous hold on serenity. (These are the people you just love to tease.)

The good news is that it is possible to overcome these traits by developing a sense of humor. Learning to laugh at yourself is the essence of a sense of humor. To do that one needs not to take himself so seriously. Telling jokes and making people laugh is called *comedy.* Both are necessary to be able to laugh—one is to have sense of humor—i.e. to be able to laugh at *oneself,* and the other, comedy, is to see the humor in the situations of life.

A sense of humor is essential for good mental and physical health. It provides balance between what is important and what is not. It allows you "not to sweat the small stuff," not to take yourself so seriously and not to be defensive.

A sense of humor is essential in intimate relationships. If couples are defensive with one another, take themselves too seriously and can't "let things go," they will have a difficult time getting along.

Here's what *lifescape.com* suggests we try:

- Choose funny TV shows, movies and books over depressing ones.
- Start the day with a comic strip instead of a headline.
- Stop waiting to be happy—try to find some pleasure in today.
- Wear something silly—mismatched socks or leopard underwear.
- Pat yourself on the back for a job well-done, even if it was merely spilling the coffee on the counter instead of yourself.
- Be grateful- say thanks to the driver who didn't hit you.
- Smile at the person next to you when you're stuck in line.
- When you trip on a rug at a meeting, don't pretend it didn't happen; make a joke even if it's corny.
- Make a joke at your own expense rather than someone else—laughing at yourself is cool, laughing at others is mean.
- Laugh at yourself, but stop short of becoming the village idiot

Under my picture in my high school yearbook, the committee wrote: Laugh and the world laughs with you. I don't remember it too well, but I guess I gave the impression that I had a good sense of humor. I'm proud about that.

Vincent B. Cardarelli, Th.M., CADC

There are times now that I wish I had that ability at my beck and call. Often enough I am known as being "too serious."

When I can laugh, then I'm happier and those around me are infected by it. And when I'm with someone who laughs I am easily drawn into it.

10. ELUSIVE SERENITY

The Inconstancy of My Attempts at Serenity

The topic of Serenity has been my focus for a long time, and it dawns on me that maybe I should "have" it by now.

The truth is that I need to keep striving both to keep it and to regain it every so often. But that's how it is: I go along feeling pretty good, "happy," saying that life is good. I am convinced that I finally got it together.

Then I wake up and I feel out of sorts, irritable, ready to complain about the unfairness of life. I feel that I have to start all over again.

Serenity is not something that once you have it, it is always there, or once you have lost it, you can't get it back.

I am reminded of a quote by the columnist Dan Savage: "In this society, we view monogamy like we view virginity—one incident and it's over, the relationship is destroyed. But we should view monogamy like sobriety...you can get sober again."

Serenity is not an all or nothing thing. "Health" is like that, too. Health is a desired goal that often enough is "lost" or threatened, only to be regained by sustained efforts.

Death, on the other hand, is a one-time thing.

Vincent B. Cardarelli, Th.M., CADC

So, in our efforts in maintaining serenity, we can't get discouraged. A person who relapses from sobriety must start over. He tries to learn from his slips and moral lapses. If you don't understand that, then you will condemn the addict by saying he is not trying. And the addict who gives up because of repeated relapses, is the same as a married person who surrenders to despair because of a wandering eye or misplaced affection.

One who loses hope in his struggles for serenity has an either-or outlook not only on serenity but probably on all aspects of his life. He/she just may be a perfectionist and become a harsh critic of himself as well as of others.

You may feel justified at condemning another's infidelity, yet feel justified at ogling a passing beauty (woman or man.) Do you lose your monogamy if you read Playboy/Playgirl? Or watch an X-rated film?

Is your serenity lost because you have a bad day? Yell at the kids? Feel demoralized?

There are innumerable factors that can affect your serenity. A situation like conflict at work is usually a biggy. You can bring it home and be grumpy at the dinner table.

A personality trait, a character defect, can for no apparent reason make you go down the emotional ladder like a roller coaster, not exactly a diagnosable illness, but upsetting nonetheless.

A low-grade fever, too much to eat or drink—you name it, there are often unexpected squalls that buffet you on your way. Hang in there until health returns. "This too shall pass." Wait until you get back to normal before you throw in the towel or make major decisions.

If you want to be monogamous, you have to "work at it." It doesn't just happen. If you want to acquire serenity, you have to work at it. It doesn't just happen.

As the prayer says: God grant me the serenity to accept the things that I can't change, the courage to change the things I can, and the wisdom to know the difference.

11. RESPONSIBILITY AND SERENITY

"The Devil Made Me Do It" Isn't a Good Enough Excuse

Geraldine was Flip Wilson's hilarious vamp, whose famous line "The Devil made me do it," was her excuse for escaping any blame or responsibility.

There is a tendency in the mental health field, as well as in the educational and court systems, to exonerate some rather weird behaviors by attributing the cause of the violations and immoralities to uncontrollable impulses and to addictions and other illnesses.

By so doing, the implication is that the person is not responsible nor at fault. For example, Richard Berendzen, who was a past president of American University, appeared on TV with a psychiatrist to explain that he was a victim, therefore blameless, of an impulse disorder which caused him to make obscene phone calls to young women.

You may remember the "Twinkie Defense"—sugar made him do it. For muggers, the reason cited could be "oppression-artifact disorder," translated means the shock of being brought up as poor-black; or as a sexually maladjusted child.

For Vietnam Vets, it is Post Traumatic Stress Syndrome. For Marion Barry, the former mayor of Washington, D.C., it is alcoholism and drug dependence.

Vincent B. Cardarelli, Th.M., CADC

For an abusive person, it would be explosive personality, which is genetically predetermined.

Who knows how far this tendency will go in the future?

Will we be so obsessed with explaining aberrant behavior that we will lose sight of the consequences? Will all offenses and abnormalities be attributed to genetics gone astray?

Although there are bona fide medical explanations for abnormal behavior, and these reasons do indeed provide an answer to why a person acts in a certain way, these diagnoses are not EXCUSES for the behavior.

If that were so, people would be able to exonerate their anti-social and harmful behavior by having recourse to a variety of disciplines, all of which nicely provide an alibi and are capable of absolving imputability.

Law, psychiatry, neurology, nutrition, genetics and sexology all have carefully worked out causative factors that explain unusual behavior. Bad habits are often not called bad habits; they can be labeled addictions, neurological hijacking of the brain, or whatever, according to the prism through which you look at the behavior.

Biological determinism is "in." Predetermined forces are so powerful as to be irresistible, and therefore these "victims" cannot be held imputable or accountable.

The implication is that the responsibility is outside of the person.

Aha! And there is the temptation. Not only do we like to explain the behavior, but we would also like to "explain *away*" the behavior, i.e., find reasons why we would not be held responsible.

Surely, it is important to find out "why" someone acts the way he does, especially when it is abnormal. But more important is "what?" i.e. what can he do about it? Even if there is a rational explanation for one's behavior, he is still responsible for that action. The responsibility may be diminished because of the reasons, but he is responsible nonetheless for what he will do about it.

Responsibility means being held accountable for yourself and for your actions, whether you are at fault or not. Illnesses and disorders which explain the behaviors are not the same as explaining away the consequences.

One who does wrong or commits a sin, or crime, although he may not be considered 'at fault', is still to be held accountable. He is responsible for what he does. No argument.

But in my business of counseling, I know that the terrain gets tricky when you talk about addictions and other psychiatric disorders. The person may not be responsible for "catching" the illness; you can't blame him for that.

But having the misfortune to contract the malady does not absolve him totally from the consequences. He is not an island unto himself; he is a member of society, and his actions do have repercussions on others. Not everyone agrees with that, so you do get an argument here.

Addictions, childhood misfortunes, or compulsions are not to be used as alibis, or excuses either in law, in school or in recovery programs. A person is still responsible. We don't have to stand in judgment over someone, but we do have to hold him responsible.

A man may be a pedophile, but that is not an excuse for molesting a child.

A parent may have a personality disorder, but that is no excuse for abusing a child.

A man may be a heavy drinker, but that is not an excuse for spending the weekly paycheck on liquor.

Sorry, Geraldine. Even if "the devil made you do it," you are still responsible for your actions.

Section II—Marriage and Relationship

1. ATTACHMENT #1

Attachment Hunger May Lead to Addictive Relationships

This is the first of three chapters on addictive, or dependent, relationships. They are an attempt to show how relationships develop, and how they affect Serenity. I think that you will see that one's serenity is jeopardized by addictive relationships, and so I won't keep referring to 'serenity' throughout these three essays. A relationship that is not satisfying makes for a roller coaster type of existence—ruining the chances of a calm, predictable union.

The aim of this article is to define "attachment hunger."

Perry Como had a hit record called "Prisoner of Love," in which he sang the words: "too weak to break the chains that bind me." Sometimes love acts like a chain that imprisons, whereas true love should release a person to fly free.

Are you a prisoner of love? Is your day and night obsessed with thoughts, longing and an aching search for your beloved? Is your compulsion to see, talk or be near your lover getting to be a "fatal attraction?"

Take Vanessa, a 47 year old woman, who had been married for 26 years and recently separated. Her husband was a womanizer, one who was verbally abusive to her and to her two children, a man who was financially irresponsible. She has been unhappy for all of her marriage, and yet she is miserable without him and could never make the decision to leave him. It was he who left her.

Or Bill. He is 25, lived with Erica for seven years while she used drugs and alcohol, and in general made his life unmanageable. She moved out to live with another man, and Bill is unable to put her out of his mind, spending time and money to keep in contact with her. He uses any specious reason to show his 'love.'

Jennifer is an 18 year old freshman in college, who has fallen for a man still in high school. He has never told her that he loves her, and in fact has done a number of things to discourage her, but she adamantly pursues him, gets herself into trouble with family, friends and the law because of her inability to let him go.

It may be that each of these suffers from *attachment hunger*.

Howard M. Halpern, author of <u>How to Break Your Addiction to A Person</u>, says that "*Attachment hunger* is the basis of being addicted to another person." He says that your attachment needs as a child to your mother did three things: 1) It kept you alive and well. 2) It gave you the illusion of being in a safe, satisfying womblike situation. 3) it gave you a sense of being powerful and able to face the world because of the close connection with a powerful person, namely your parent(s).

There is a period of a child's life when he necessarily forms a close, emotional attachment to his mother. Two aspects of this developmental need (called attachment) must play themselves out. The first is that the child must experience a feeling of being connected and protected by a safe and reliable person. To have this person always available to you as a child allowed you to face the rest of the world without fear. If your attachment need is not adequately fulfilled in childhood, then it may surface in later life and be expressed by anxiety and clinging behavior.

The second aspect of attachment need that a child should experience is the feeling of being "launched" away from the harbor of a safe person at the appropriate time. In other words, not only does your parent provide you with security by the symbiotic closeness, but your parent also "lets you go," or launches you at the right time, so that you don't have to "hold on," or "come back home" to feel secure and face the world with courage.

To feel safe within yourself, and to be launched with confidence into the world finishes the work of attachment. You begin to feel that you can stand on your own two feet, that you are a person in your own right.

If as a child my separation from my parents was fraught with fear and insecurity, if I needed to "check out" all my decisions, or get an OK from someone above, then I may very well repeat the pattern with a lover. I will need constant reassurance that my relationship with him/her is safe. The threat of losing the person will trigger panic, anger and clinging behavior. No cost is too great to maintain the attachment, and breaking off the relationship is very difficult.

This is what Halpern calls the *"hangover of attachment hunger."* It's like a memory of that unresolved period of your life; you may experience an intense *hangover*, a hungry search to fill an empty space within, and it seems that the only thing that can satisfy that hunger is the other person.

As a result, you will feel a compelling urge to seek and to cling to relationships in an addictive way. It is almost like a flashback urge to recreate and recapture the strength, security and bliss that comes from fusing with another person.

You will get a high from the nearness of the other person, no matter how destructive the relationship might be.

It is not easy to explain or to understand this compulsion (addiction). *Attachment hunger* is a basic, primal need, that, if frustrated in early life, will have a strong sub-conscious effect on all relationships in later life.

2. ATTACHMENT #2

Attachment Hunger Can Lead to Addictive Relationships

This is the second of three chapters on addictive relationships.

The first one showed how *attachment hunger is the basis of being addicted to another person.* Briefly, the pattern of forming attachments (relationships) is set with a child's parents. If the pattern was healthy, chances are that later relationships will be healthy. But if the pattern was unhealthy, then an *attachment hunger* is triggered with subsequent relationships.

We experience an attachment hunger when someone comes into our lives who re-enkindles feelings of dependency similar to those we had with our parents. When another person becomes important to us, lover or not, then we react instinctively: we desire (hunger) closeness and seek to cling (attach) to that person.

Most of the time, the attachments we form are healthy and normal. That is how relationships begin, and they lead to partnerships and marriages that are satisfying.

Sometimes, however, we may repeat an unhealthy pattern that we learned as a child, and then the *attachment hunger* takes over, thus forming an unhealthy union. In a sense, I don't take a partner, I take a hostage. That's because an addictive attachment is obsessive and controlling. One can't let go, and the thoughts and preoccupations overflow into the major part of one's day. One seeks to control the life of the other, and in turn is controlled by the other.

Such a relationship can be destructive and extremely upsetting, not only to the partners, but also to the family as well. The relationship is based on maintaining an illusion: namely, that "I have to keep this relationship at all costs; if I lose it, I myself will be lost." Fear and panic accompany any threat to the relationship.

Down deep, one realizes that it is not good, and so he needs to rationalize the union into being something that it surely is not. Although everyone around us knows it to be wrong and exaggerated, nevertheless one needs to hang on to the illusion.

Keeping alive the attachment with the loved one (feeding the hunger) becomes the single most important goal in the addicted one's life. It becomes compulsive to control the circumstances of the relationship, because he can not let it get away from him.

One way to control the other is through **power**: "Do it my way, or else..." This is followed by a threat. The most powerful threat is that of **loss**: "I will leave, or get a divorce." Another threat is suicide.

Still another is to become **bratty, or demanding,** like a child who tyrannizes, embarrasses or dominates his parents.

Guilt is an effective control. A child who formed his attachments with a *Martyr Mother,* may be easily manipulated as an adult by a spouse who uses **blame** and **guilt** as tools to get what he wants. "How can you be so selfish?" "It's all your fault."

Halpern (q.v.) says: "When *attachment hunger* rules your feelings and your actions, it can cause powerful bodily and emotional reactions that can override your judgment, distort your perceptions of time and people, and shape your feelings about yourself. It is at the base of your addictive ties to other people."

Vincent B. Cardarelli, Th.M., CADC

But *attachment hunger* need not be destructive. In fact, a healthy dose of it is at the base of a spiritual quest for oneness with God. It is at the base of a person's seeking a true love. It is a motive that spurs political rallies, song fests and drug-induced states, all of which can create feelings of connection, one-ness, solace, security and what Halpern calls "limerance." More about this in the next chapter.

However, when the relationship is all-consuming, then the decision whether or not to end it can be the most agonizing one that a person has to face. Is the gratification of an addictive relationship worth paying the price of anxiety, panic and fear?

Let's talk about that next time in the third and last of this series.

3. ATTACHMENT #3

There is Hope for Addictive Relationships

    I think there are more young people these days who fall into addictive relationships than in the past. Addictive relationships are ones which are controlling and possessive; they are caused by *attachment hunger.* The last two essays defined what that means; this chapter seeks to show that one does not need to capture and control his partner in order to be safe and happy.
    Youthful attractions used to be called *puppy love,* or *going steady*—words which showed the passing nature of the attraction. But now, they are called "relationships" or "they are a couple," which have more serious implications. So serious, in fact, that we are seeing violence to the point of murder when the relationship is ended. News reports covered a rejected eighth grader who killed a teacher on his way to get even with his girl-friend.
    There are two ways to look at an addictive relationship. The first way is healthy in the sense that a person, at whatever age, experiences what some authors call "limerance," a romantic love, a blissful state of being high, a vision of the loved one as utterly wonderful and perfect. There is an excitement, a sense of safety in the committed connection. The experience of falling in love is one of

intense oneness that causes a "rush" of endorphins—a rush that one seeks to repeat over and over again.

The second way (unhealthy) to look at it is in the sense that there is a heavy price to pay for addictive relationships. Most expensive are the obsessive thoughts which intrude into all parts of one's life. Another is the need to control the behavior of the loved one, thus becoming possessive.

"Where are you? Why didn't you call?"

Then too, one experiences a constant fear of loss, which produces an anxiety that is alleviated only by the presence of the other person. The addict suffers a continual, stifling, demanding, insistent urge to be with the beloved.

Sooner or later, addictive love exacts too great a price, and the lover has no other choice but to end it. It ends up being a self-fulfilling prophecy; the very thing that the addict tries to prevent is the thing that he causes to happen.

I'm not sure that we can prevent such relationships from developing, but we can learn to heal them when a couple finds themselves so affected. And *healing* is the correct word because they are so unhealthy. Here are some suggestions:

First, *examine your beliefs and values.* Do you want your relationship to be permanent, and do you think this one will be? Do you really need someone else to be *complete*, or can you manage on your own if you had to? Does *love* really conquer all?

Besides the infatuation that you feel so strongly, what other things do you have in common? How does he (she) treat **ME**?

Repeat to yourself some daily reminders: Love does not conquer all. A relationship should be mutual. I trust him—he trusts me. I feel calm in his presence (or not!). I don't feel pressured to check up on him (her) all the time.

Second, *use some practical methods* to view your relationship objectively. Keep a journal of your times together and how you interact, so that you can remember what price you pay for the joys that you reap. It will also remind you not to make the same mistakes over and over. Nurture several friends to whom you can confide, who understand and will listen without getting impatient.

Get some help for the two of you to communicate better, and to break the patterns that lead to arguments.

Third, *examine your attachment hunger* and to what extent it affects the way you form your relationships. You can learn to be aware of your attachment needs and stop yourself from acting or making decisions based on unresolved attachment hunger. Watch our for dependency needs which are expressed by clinging behavior.

If you believe that you can stand on your own two feet, then you can convince yourself that you can NOT resolve it, and you can only let it go and say "goodbye."

Especially, **listen** to your feelings. If you find yourself often irritated, and doing things against your will, examine your attachment needs, and see if the *hunger* is too strong.

Howard Halpern (q.v.) says: "You can satisfy your attachment hunger through an intimate relationship. (But) if you find that your attachment needs have led you into bad relationships, the answer is not in giving up on relationships or in trying to deny your *attachment hunger.* The answer is in changing your old self-defeating patterns of fulfilling your attachment hunger to self-enhancing ways of fulfilling it." You need to "form relationships which satisfy your attachment needs in a supportive rather than a destructive (dependent) way."

When you find yourself in a relationship that gratifies both the "adolescent" as well as the "adult" part of you, then you will find quiet, satisfying companionship. It will be a serene couple-ship. Watch out for the panicky, needy, clinging, possessive and insecure relationships!

4. INFATUATION

Or The Chemical Hijacking of the Brain

Infatuation is the first step in the formation of a close relationship. For many people, however, it is often the only step they want, or are able, to take. That's unfortunate, because the experience of infatuation, as intoxicating as it is, is just the first step—the doorway, as it were, to a lasting relationship.

Infatuation is powerfully euphoric; it produces an intense high. The word *infatuation* describes a state of bliss that is delirious and sexually exciting. It is like a bewitching siren that beckons a man to a woman, or a woman to a man. Infatuation is full of energy, causing the one who is washed away by it to overcome all obstacles to be united (sexually) to the other.

Sometimes, if one becomes infatuated with a married person, the power and energy of the passion will blind the person to the possible harm and danger that can result.

We all know of prominent men and women who jeopardize career and family almost in a blind, compulsive way. Logic and common sense don't seem to have any effect. And there is a good reason for that kind of reckless behavior!

The reason is that infatuation is caused by a brain bath of naturally occurring amphetamines that pool in the emotional center of the brain. When a certain person comes along, the chemical factory of the body wakes up and produces a stimulant rush. It's called *phenylethylamine* (PEA), a natural neurotransmitter that acts just like the drug amphetamine. This flooding causes a feeling of ecstasy—one is *smitten!*

That reaction sets up a compulsion to repeat the experience, and so the man/woman will do anything to reunite. Remember the teacher who couldn't stay away from her young, student lover, even after she got out of jail? Everyone was asking: "What's the matter with her?" For her there seemed to be no choice; her brain was *hijacked!* by PEA.

The brain produces PEA in reaction to the presence, thought or desire of the loved one. PEA is then produced by the body for a period of about three or four years. It is surmised by researchers that this is a "survival" mechanism in the evolutionary process, and its purpose is to keep couples who are thus attracted to one another together long enough to produce and care for their children.

The crippling passion of infatuation leads to attachment as described in previous chapters, which is a deep closeness, a kind of serenity and peace that comes from knowing that someone is "there," from knowing that "I belong." It is the feeling of "two are made one." Infatuation starts the search; attachment ends the search. You are fulfilled.

Attachment, also called bonding, is what happens between an infant and his mother, between friends in adolescence, and between lovers when they are infatuated with one another.

It is infatuation that gets it all started. It is the fireworks of a relationship and after the initial flare, it settles into attachment. Infatuation can be recaptured periodically by vacations, going off to a romantic spot, etc.

Vincent B. Cardarelli, Th.M., CADC

It is the stuff of spicy novels, newspaper articles and scandal sheets. Tragic, like "Looking for Mr. Goodbar;" gossipy, like older man, younger woman; hopeful, like a second marriage; scandalous, like an adulterous affair.

Infatuation is not secure or confident, and it is not meant to be. Ann Landers says: "When he's away, you wonder if he's cheating. Sometimes you check. You must have him right away. You can't risk losing him."

Infatuation is a means to an end; by itself it does not produce serenity. It leads to attachment, if true love follows, and then to a stable, confident relationship. However, when infatuation is an end in itself, the "high" is as far as it goes, and then it can become as addicting as cocaine, and just as hard to break.

5. INSURANCE POLICY

Vince's Four-Part Insurance Policy for a Healthy Marriage

A large percentage of my practice is spent in marriage counseling. And most of the sessions with couples deal with communication—how to talk and how to listen. Not an easy task.

They say that art imitates life, or is it that life imitates art. Either way, the modern art forms are not good examples of effective communication. For example, the love songs of The Beatles, or the ballads of Sinatra were understandably more effective at getting the message across; but modern music is loud, repetitive and hard to understand, both the words as well as the meaning. Is it that the art imitates life? Or vice versa? Or take the commercials—all sound bites, quick and pithy. Or the sitcom's type of comedy—satire, silly, and adolescent.

It is difficult for married couples to find models of good communication around them. Later chapters describe "The Four Horsemen of Divorce: Criticism, Defensiveness, Contempt and Withdrawal." Some couples easily resort to this kind of communication, and when they do, they are harbingers of divorce. Communication interspersed with the four horsemen does not foster harmony or union.

Vincent B. Cardarelli, Th.M., CADC

How does a couple stay together in this day and age? Are there any strategies that will insure their marriage against the Four Horsemen?

I recommend a four-point "insurance policy" for couples who come for therapy. I think it is good for any couple. The four points are based on my conviction that when communication is effective, it is also unifying; after all, that is what the word means: "to be in union with." Good communication produces a "high" that is refreshing and calming; it generates endorphins.

The *art* of talking and the *art* of listening allow the couple to form a unity, a "communion." Like any other "high" there rises a compulsion to repeat the experience.

People are willing to pay because I "listen" well. I don't judge, I don't guess at the meaning, or interrupt or jump to conclusions. They feel better (endorphins are released) when they experience understanding. And if I don't understand, I make them repeat what they said until I do understand. It takes time, and a quiet determination, but the experience is rewarding.

My "insurance policy" seeks to have couples create the same atmosphere at home with one another that exists in my office—with a stranger.

There are four rules or guidelines to the policy. In the beginning, be diligent and scrupulous in following them. It is difficult to do, and much easier to fall back on the old habits. But try it.

Rule No 1. Set aside one-half hour at least once a week. Pick a time, such as Sunday morning, or later at night, before the activity starts, or after it has ended. One couple who had eight children put aside the time before dinner once or twice a week, when he came home from work. They called it the 'happy hour' and the children knew they were not to be disturbed.

Observe the time set-aside faithfully because it is important. Just like the worship hour for a religious family, you do it even when on vacation, or when there is something else that may tempt you away.

Rule No. 2. No one or nothing must interrupt that time. No phone calls, no children calling for help, no business or work. This time is *yours and mine.*

Rule No. 3. Use the rules for "fighting fair." I describe those rules in another chapter, Fighting fair applies to arguments and solving problems, as well as to differing perceptions about the same event. But I also suggest that you use the same directives during the half-hour to show interest and caring. Here's a short review of how to fight fair:

- **Take turns.** One speaks while the other listens. No exceptions. When the first spouse (he or she) talks, he does so until he has finished his thought. Then he says "I'm finished."
- **Do not interrupt.** The other spouse waits until she hears the words "I'm finished," and then she has her turn. How tempting it is for the listener to pick out some word, some nuance, some incorrect fact, and jump in before the speaker is finished. That is where communication usually breaks down. So don't interrupt. Wait until the other is finished.

  When communication does break down, the couple has recourse to one of the four horsemen of divorce: criticism defensiveness, contempt or withdrawal. **Do not interrupt.** This is the key to good communication skills.
- **No vulgarity or threats.** That means you need to avoid incendiary words and threatening actions like waving your hands or pointing your finger. It means that must look for acceptable ways to express what are disagreeable thoughts and feelings. You will improve your vocabulary, and you'll show respect for your partner.

Vincent B. Cardarelli, Th.M., CADC

Rule No. 4. Plan a weekend away and alone. Do this at least four times a year.

More often if you both have high-stress jobs. Well, you say, we don't even talk in the car when we go someplace. True. But when you have an extended period together, you force yourselves to come up with things to talk about and to do together. Then practice the rules of fighting fair, which will force you to pay attention to one another.

You are also away from the stressors and distractions, and are able to see one another in a more natural state. Memories are stirred up of when you were courting.

Some couples resort to getting away when their marriage is beyond repair in the hopes of salvaging it. I suggest you get away to nurture your marriage rather than repair it.

Those are the four rules that constitute my "insurance policy" that protects the marriage. The four rules lead to good communication, which in turn leads to a "high" or an enjoyment in being together. These are the requirements of greater intimacy.

I believe that what I can create in my office, namely, a spirit of understanding, is a climate you can also create at home. Why pay for it, when by following the four rules you can do it without cost?

6. FIGHT FAIR

An Invitation to Fight—but Fight Fair

I'd like to extend an invitation to couples to fight, to get angry, and to express your anger to one another, and especially to the one you love. But I want you to "fight fair," not just fight in your usual manner.

To fight fair, you need to believe that anger is a good emotion. It has been given to you to help you purify your love for one another. You don't get angry at someone that you don't care about or love. It is a legitimate human emotion which is meant to set limits, to protect yourself, and to let others know when you are excited or inflamed about something. It is a primary tool in the art of communication.

Here are six statements you can mull over, and discuss with your partner:

- It is O.K. to feel anger.
- You have the right to express that anger.
- You also have the right to *repress* anger.
- It is not so healthy to *suppress* anger—i.e. be totally unaware that you are angry.
- Saying "NO" quietly and firmly to someone, even to someone you love, is an expression of anger.

- Don't take ownership of someone else's anger—you are not responsible for it.

What do you think about these statements? They are the principles of anger management, and if you have any problem with any of these principles, then you probably have a problem with anger. You need to be comfortable with each of them in order to "fight fair."

There are various degrees of anger, from passive on one end of the spectrum to aggressive, or violent, on the other end. In between there are numerous hues and colors: irritation, assertiveness, belligerence, seething and sulking, walking away in frustration, etc. The appropriate use of anger means that you are able to pick out the right amount to do the job needed. No need to yell and scream when a simple "no" will do the trick. No need to use a sledge hammer when a fly swatter is sufficient.

Let me divert for a moment to point out that anger and resentment are not the same. Resentment means past anger that was stuffed and/or never expressed, and as a result never resolved. It is "baggage" that one carries around and that interferes with serenity. Resentment leads to the "Four Horsemen" of divorce: criticism, defensiveness, contempt and withdrawal. More about these four in another chapter. Resentment needs to be let go; it has to be flushed away, just like a stopped up drain. "Let Go and Let God" says the AA adage.

I am convinced that there is no resolution for resentment except for letting it go, or forgiving the one against whom the resentment is directed.

To get back to the main point: There is *no resolution without confrontation.* That means that if two people are at loggerheads—disagreement, hurt, thoughtlessness, - the only way to resolve it is to lay the cards on the table, to confront the issue. The argument or division causes anger to arise, and so one needs to know how to manage that anger. Anger is the motor, the energy that drives me to express what it is that riles me up. But it should be expressed under the control of the rational mind. The mind is like the steering wheel guiding the motor. Like any other emotion that runs amuck, runaway anger will cause more harm than good.

So, to repeat, I invite you to fight, but to FIGHT FAIR.

Try this exercise next time you get angry at something your spouse did or said. The rules for this exercise are:

First, you say; **Let's fight fair.** That will alert your partner that something is in the air that needs clarification.

Then **you sit facing one another,** making an effort to look at one another. You may not use your hands such as waving them around or pointing, since that can be intimidating. Make it fair

Take turns making your point. Like baseball, one is at bat, while the other is in the field. You can't both be talking at the same time. So while one is talking, DO NOT INTERRUPT! That's essential! Wait until your partner says: **I'm finished.** Then it's your turn, and end by saying "I'm finished."

Continue back and forth...until the fight runs out of gas, or until there is some kind of resolution, or compromise or postponement.

Fighting Fair is an exercise and a learning tool to express anger to another and to receive anger in return. You begin to learn that anger is not rejection; it is a cleansing agent in a relationship. It is something like a debate, but instead of ideas or opinions, emotions are expressed. There is no winner or loser. It is "fair" because the bigger or louder partner can't dominate by interrupting and thus "win." Each one has an equal chance—a chance of talking and a chance of being listened to.

You may need a referee for the first few sessions—and that is where counseling might help.

Don't resort to the "four horsemen." Fight fair instead. Get used to anger. I invite you to fight—but fight fair.

7. VINDICATION IS NOT THE SAME AS SERENITY

I think you'll find it interesting to know how some of the ideas for this book originated. Sometimes it is an article in the paper, sometimes people ask for a certain theme, and sometimes two or three things happen that dovetail into a thought.

In the case of this essay, it was the coming together of two things. One was that I was thinking about the topic of "vindication" and its connection to serenity.

Vindication is a distinct feeling, but serenity is not so much an identifiable feeling separate from other feelings, but rather a state of being in which all one's feelings work harmoniously.

Now there are many *good* or *positive* feelings, as opposed to *bad* feelings. The list is long: joy, satisfaction, freedom, triumph, intimacy, etc. And vindication is one of these good feelings.

As I was mulling over what I wanted to write, a second thing happened. In one of my sessions, I met Mr. G who came to "acquire some serenity." I asked what he thought he needed to work on and in the course of answering, he said this: "It's important to have everyone see things MY way. My *rightness* has to recognized."

In other words, he needed to be vindicated. And there was the genesis of my essay.

TOWARD SERENITY

I think you'll agree that people express their vindication in numerous ways. "I told you so!" "See, I was right all along." "Just wait until you have your own children."

"If only you had listened to me."

That's what vindication sounds like. Vindication is justifying oneself especially in the light of later developments. It is gathering proof that one is right, morally and factually right. When events prove that one is right, the need is satisfied, and one feels vindicated: and that is a good feeling.

To feel vindicated is to feel like hitting a home run, or winning a spelling bee.

To feel vindicated feels like "Aha! See what I have done, and how good I am."

Most of the time, it is a justifiable feeling and causes no harm. It is like pinning a medal on your lapel.

But sometimes it can be carried too far. When one not only wins a point, or has been proven right, then goes on to *rejoice* in the shame or loss that another experiences, then it is more like rubbing it in.

Also when, like my friend, one always **must** be right and needs to have that rightness recognized, then trouble brews.

In a relationship, if one needs to be right in any disagreement, then the other person will either get angry (frustrated) or will withdraw. (Fight or flight).

"Well, you could have saved yourself a lot of heartache if you had only done it MY way." This kind of vindication comes at a great price. It is called a Pyrrhic victory, a victory that is offset by staggering losses. I win the battle but lose the war.

The Pope recently publicly apologized for the injustices committed in the past by the Catholic Church. Many will feel vindicated, and justly so.

But vindication is not the same as serenity.

Victims can be vindicated for the injustices committed against them, and yet never achieve serenity. A wife who

Vincent B. Cardarelli, Th.M., CADC

has been abused for a long time can get her day in court, yet that by itself will not bring serenity. Neither will vindication bring serenity for Bosnians, Jews, Palestinians, children of slaves, or adult children of abusive parents.

Yet, having said that, there is certainly a place for vindication. Even the Bible says that the Lord will even the score: "Vengeance is mine, saith the Lord."

But substituting vindication for serenity is like a sultry temptress. The more you get the more you want. You have to keep "winning" in order to feel *good*. Whereas serenity make you feel good whether you win or lose.

It is certainly important for victims to have their day in court and be vindicated. But in a family, the need for vindication has to take a very low priority. Between husband and wife, between parents and children, between friend and friend—priority #1 is to live in harmony. So instead of win-lose, we need to arrive at a win-win situation. Or at least at a no-lose one.

Instead of asking who's right, we need to ask different questions. Like: How do families resolve differing perceptions of the same event? How do we get along even if we see things differently?

What's the good of being vindicated if we still bear our grudges? Like any game in which winning is the goal, the process becomes addictive, because we keep on trying to win as proof of something...but of what?

"I win" is different from "I'm at peace with myself and my family." Both experiences produce "good" feelings, but the feelings are not the same.

In the case of Mr. G, he wants to learn how to "let go of my need to win," and wants to have a more relaxed and intimate relationship with those whom he loves.

8. VENTILATE, VALIDATE, BUT DON'T VINDICATE

Part I

In the previous chapter, I showed that Vindication is not the same as Serenity. In this one, I'd like to continue the idea and apply it to the art of communicating. And communicating IS an art—it is not something that "comes naturally." What *does* come naturally is the urge to *win.* When talking to another, there is a strong desire to vindicate one's point of view, to prove that one is *right.*

For example, I am writing this during the political conventions, and surely, each party needs to be vindicated in November. One will win, and one will lose. It is important to be vindicated; but vindication is NOT communication.

To communicate means to share ideas, opinions, feelings and experiences with someone. It is one of the joys of life; in fact, it is one of the greatest joys. The ability to communicate is essential to a relationship. But be careful, because if you wish to communicate (not simply converse) with another, you must avoid vindication.

Remember the days of courting—when you were with your *innamorata,* it was important to listen and to please her (him). It was not so important to make a point, or to win an argument. And the reason that you were so dedicated to the other, was that you wanted to have her like you; you wanted

Vincent B. Cardarelli, Th.M., CADC

to become more intimate. And so, you fashioned your words and the expression of your words into what would please her, attract her, and not alienate yourself.

After all, if she (he) got ticked off, your chances of having a pleasant, affectionate evening were jeopardized.

You were able to postpone gratification (most of the time), because of the prize at the end. You were willing to wait, if you wanted something. If you gave her an invitation to a dinner, or to a movie, and she had to "get back to you," you didn't take your marbles and go home in a snit. You knew you had to back off for awhile, and play your cards right.

That's called "purposeful behavior," that is, behavior that has a definite goal as its end. It is also thoughtful behavior—namely, you are thinking of the other before yourself, and monitoring what you will say so that it will not be thoughtlessly harmful. Your communication, you knew instinctively, had to be purposeful and thoughtful.

The point is that you had to make an effort if you wanted to communicate effectively. It didn't come naturally. To emphasize that point, I'd remind you that if you did *what comes naturally* when you were courting, you would go immediately to intimate behavior (the bedroom). You would "score." But you knew that if you did that you would jeopardize the end result. You would strike out. So you learned the art of postponing gratification.

But once the barrier was crossed, then "familiarity breeds contempt" as they say. And with time you go back to doing what comes naturally, and forgetting that communicating is an art and needs to be practiced continually.

To communicate means to have a union of minds and hearts as its goal. "Communicate" comes from two Latin words that means "with" (cum) and "union" (unione)—to be in union with. To want to communicate is purposeful behavior.

Vindication (see previous chapter: Vindication is Not the Same as Serenity) means to win an argument. It means to prove a point, and to sit in triumph. It means that after a disagreement with my spouse, I am proven right by later events.

And so, in order to communicate effectively, you need to avoid vindication, not 100% of the time, but at least when something important is being discussed. It is during those times that you would do well to *Ventilate and Validate* instead of *Vindicate.*

This chapter is the first of two on the topic of V & V (ventilate and validate). In the next one, I'll write about "how to" V & V. Please turn the page.

9. VENTILATE AND VALIDATE; DON'T VINDICATE

Part II

Father Brown was my Elocution teacher in the Seminary. He taught us the art of preaching. He emphasized that there were three purposes of preaching: *docere,* which means to teach; *movere,* to motivate to action; and *placere,* to please or entertain. That really sums up what the purposes are when there is one-way communication.

After all, that is what preaching is—a one-sided verbal presentation.

But *communication* is not preaching; it is a two-way connection. Two people making "presentations" of one to the other in an effort to make an intimate connection by use of words.

When I got up in the pulpit, no one ever talked back. The congregation gave me permission to do all the talking. But when I got married and sat around the table, then what I had to say was only part of what needed to happen. What my wife had to say was equally important; so I had to learn TO LISTEN, as well as to speak.

What?! You mean that what you have to say is just as important as what I have to say? Well, guess what? The answer is yes.

Communication is not as easy as preaching; preaching is an ART but so is communication. It is an art that needs to be practiced.

An effective method to practice communication is called *ventilate and validate.* I'll describe what it is, first, then I'll apply it to several situations.

Ventilate means to put your thought and feelings into words. *Validate* means to repeat in your own words what the other has said. Partners in communication take turns in ventilating and validating. First, partner #1 ventilates; partner #2 listens, but does not interrupt. #1 then says: I'm finished. Then partner #2 reflects back what he heard. If he has heard accurately, it then becomes his turn to ventilate and #1 listens without interrupting.

Rules are simple. #1 ventilates and says: I'm finished. #2 listens, does not interrupt and validates by repeating the message. Then they alternate. #2 ventilates; #1 listens and validates; no interrupting. If the validation is not accurate—in other words, if the validator did not understand, then #1 says it again, until understanding is attained.

Then the roles are reversed, and the process is repeated. It's like baseball. When one is up at bat, the other is in the field. Both can't be "at bat" at the same time. This is not like football where both are "attacking" at the same time. To communicate effectively, a couple must take turns.

It sounds simple enough. But the one who is ventilating needs to take the time to say what he means and mean what he says. Sometimes, in the rush to beat the interruption, he ventilates an incomplete thought. The knowledge that he won't be interrupted allows the ventilator to take his time.

On the other side, it looks like it's easy enough for the validator to "listen". But often the one who is "listening" is in reality preparing a rebuttal, and is off in his own head, not really paying attention to what his partner is saying. The willingness to feed-back what he heard, forces him to pay attention.

Vincent B. Cardarelli, Th.M., CADC

At first, this process feels mechanical and stilted. But with practice it gives great satisfaction to both partners, to the one who receives understanding and to the one who gives understanding. It's reminiscent of their courting days, when through thoughtfulness and purposeful behavior each was intent on pleasing the other.

When to use V & V? It's pretty clear that you can't use this method all the time. But when a disagreement arises, or when one or the other gets irritated, or is the throes of some emotion, I then recommend V & V as the method of communication that will work.

When one or both are having "positive" feelings—affection, humor, success and the like—you don't need to "practice" any so-called method to communicate. But when harsh or what are called negative emotions need to be expressed, then I suggest that you reach into your bag of tricks and trot out V & V.

Try it when attempting communication with your children. Let them talk; don't interrupt. Reflect back what you heard. Let them correct what you misheard. Then ask them for the same respect—for you to be heard by *them.*

It is so tempting to resort to "preaching" with the kids. Try putting yourself on the same level as they.

It's a way of fighting fair, in the sense that no one has an advantage because of size or strength or personality. V & V makes for a level playing field—like baseball.

Try it out.

10. RELATIONSHIPS NEED TO REACH FOR A NEW LEVEL

Relationships need commitment, patience and an ability to postpone instant gratification. As they say, "you need to work on it." But modern relationships need something more—they need to reach for a new level between couples.

New gadgets are constantly being created for age-old tasks: e.g. a kitchen appliance can be started through a digital phone. And so I propose here a 'new" technique for the modern relationship. Books by Deborah Tannen and John Gray, and many others, have been written about this topic.

As the roles for men and women have changed, so also the nature of the relationship between them needs to change. For the cave man, it was enough to grunt to make his intentions known. As time went on, men and women fell into roles that satisfied the times they were in. Men were called upon to fight and protect; women had to tend and befriend.

Now, however, it is evident that "old ways" are not working. Women are becoming more independent as providers and protectors of themselves. Men are called upon to be more emotionally supportive of wives and family rather than simply problem solvers. And so, we need to evolve into a new level or relating.

As an example, we have seen the sexual revolution of women in the past fifty years, and that is just a prelude of the evolution that women will experience in the future. That phenomenon has already had an effect on men. More romance will be expected both from men as well as from women; women won't be able to 'have a headache' as often, and will have to learn how to communicate their needs to men in a way their grandmothers never had to. Men won't have the excuse of being the strong silent type, incapable of expressing their feelings.

I think the most important "new" tool to learn for couples is to *communicate on a new level.* "Ventilate and Validate," is the "new" tool.

Communication has traditionally been used to a) pass along information; b) to share experiences and feelings: c) to solve problems: d) to give an opinion or pass judgment on something or someone.

We still need to do those things with the words that we use. But we need something more when it comes to relationships; "ventilate and validate" (V & V) is the doorway to that goal. V&V is a tool used to "hear" and "be heard" (See Section II, Chapters 6, 8, & 9)

A great part of my work is to use words. To me words are worth more than pictures, especially to nurture relationships. So it is important to be thoughtful in picking out the words that you throw at your loved ones. Think about this:

Words are chemical. MRI's show that words have a physiological impact on the brain, just as much as Prozac. Parts of the brain light up in response to words indicating the kind of effect produced. Since the brain is the control panel, it triggers emotional reactions of highs and lows. Thoughtful communication causes "highs." Whereas criticism and belittling cause "lows."

Why rely on medicine to produce good feelings when we have at our disposal a technique just as powerful as any medicine? When I train couples to V & V, they FEEL BETTER!

So it makes sense to train ourselves to communicate with this "new" technique: V & V is that technique.

In the future, men will be invited to become better lovers, more romantic and more understanding. Women will be better able to communicate their real needs to men, and not be critical of male ineptitude; they won't have to be in competition with men.

Through V & V couples will enjoy sitting down and sharing themselves with one another. They will not be afraid to fight with one another, as long as they 'fight fair.' As John Gray, author of *Women are from Venus, Men from Mars* says, "We will continue to set new and higher standards of what defines a fully romantic and sexually rewarding relationship."

By continuing to sharpen our communication skills, couples will be able to sustain relationships 20, 30, and 40 years into marriage. Romance does not have to die when courtship ends and marriage begins.

11. EXPECTATIONS AND MARRIAGE

Serenity in Marriage Depends on Curbing Expectations

It's a truism to say that serenity depends on whether one perceives that he has a happy marriage, and on whether he hopes that it will last "forever."

What I plan to write here is not about the sociology of marriage; on what it is supposed to be, or what the purposes of a union between man and woman are; or what the differences are between the marriages of 50 years ago and those of today.

These are some random thoughts from the point of view of a therapist who has tried for years to help couples make their relationship work.

John Gray, author of <u>Men Are From Mars, Women Are From Venus</u>, has written at least five books on relationships. FIVE! Do we have to read all that much to do it right? Besides that, he had been married to Barbara DeAngelis, who herself has written books on relationships and happiness. They were divorced. Then they remarried and now seem to be doing it right. Do we need to practice marriage at least once in order to learn how to live with another?

Maybe the many volumes that are written say that marriage TODAY is more complicated than it used to be. Just like writing e-mail is more complicated than writing a letter via Pony Express.

Incidentally, many of the books on marriage and on relationships, as well as self-help books, have been written by divorced men and women. One thing seems certain, that there is no one right way to do marriage. There are a lot of different types of marriages. I knew a couple who were married for 64 years. He was definitely the boss, and she the subservient one. It worked for them. I have friends each of whom has a career and do not want children. It has lasted for 20 years at last counting. Another couple are in their 70's; the wife was an early feminist, breaking new ground, like Eleanor Roosevelt. Their relationship has worked for almost 50 years.

But I also see couples who have tried for a long time to make it work and just couldn't do it.

As I do my work (hard but satisfying) with today's couples, I see every variation that you can think of; some of them work and some don't. And I don't know why. Yes, we all have theories about it, but the theories do not make or break marriages. People do. Couples do.

My father had a corner grocery store in the '40's. He was a good man, he extended credit to those who could not pay. He never refused food for the poor and the children who needed it. But he did not have what it took to be a business man. While his friends, immigrants like he, went on to be wealthy and influential in business, he went bankrupt in 1945. His lack of ability in business did not reflect on his character or his morality. Some have it and some do not. No one ever condemned him.

And you know what? I don't think he ever could have learned the skills that were needed to "make it."

In some ways, I think it is like that in marriage, except for the fact that there are many out there who do condemn couples who can't make it.

People bare their souls to me, just like confession. Some seem to have what it takes to relearn instinctual habits

Vincent B. Cardarelli, Th.M., CADC

of a lifetime and make effective adjustments. Others do not, no matter what techniques, beliefs and motivation I try to employ. I see very few who are intentionally dishonest or insincere; so it is not that. Everyone wants to be happy, serene. Everyone comes with high hopes.

As different as every couple is, however, there is one characteristic common to all—at least initially. Each partner wants the other to change; wants the other to live up to his/her expectations. Each has formed in his/her own mind the kind of partner he expected to have, and he/she does this subconsciously. The words: "If only..." represent this desire. "*If only* he were to...*If only*...she would." In other words, there would be no problem *if only* my partner would change. The problem is not IN HERE, it is OUT THERE.

Each partner has an urge to tell the other how to live. Be reasonable, do it my way. Initially, each of us wants the other to see the world through his eyes. After trying to make "John" see her point of view, "Jane" in exasperation said "You may be right, John." And he countered without blinking an eyelash: "Of course, I'm right."

And whenever one says *If only* about someone else, it is an expectation. "*If only* you would make a list, everything would be fine." The expectation is that the other should become more organized.

But when I say *if only* about myself, then it becomes a challenge and an obligation. For example, *if only* I could let go of my resentments and hurts, instead of nursing them and seeking retaliation, then I would be able to be comfortable around you.

If only I would be willing to give more of myself, then I could say:
    If my marriage cannot 50-50 be
    Let who gives the major part be me.

If only I could learn to make some changes while I am still married instead of waiting for the second time around.

From the point of view of a therapist, expectations often prevent a person from accepting what his partner is really like. It is one the first things that couples need to look at.

12. COMPROMISE AND MARRIAGE

Simple to Envision but Tough to Carry Out

I saw a cartoon in which the Ziggy character stood in front of a display window with a large sign which said: "If you don't see what you want lower your expectations." You will attain more serenity if you can manage your own expectations—not give them up, mind you,—but manage them and make them more realistic.

That was the point of the previous chapter on Marriage and Serenity. Following are a few thoughts on the importance of compromise as a tool for serenity.

The solution of any problem between two people is most often a compromise. A compromise is the settlement of a disagreement by mutual concessions. Neither side wins, but both sides accommodate and adapt. Neither gets the whole pie; each one gets a piece of the pie. AND is HAPPY to do it. That's the catch. Each is happy because they care about each other.

How easy it is to carry a grudge about giving something up, and then later on, look to even the score. The hardest part of the compromise is to accept the concession.

If one or both do not accept the compromise, what you have is an armed truce that can reignite at any moment. And the result of that is to try to "win," to score a point against your partner (read: adversary). Scoring points is O.K. for a competitive ball game where you do have an opponent, but it is lethal for the cooperation needed in a relationship. A real compromise makes both partners happy, makes for peace; the acrimony dissipates.

An example: John, an alcoholic, is married to Mary. Now, we all know that living with alcoholism affects the behavior of both spouses. The alcoholic becomes progressively irresponsible. The spouse becomes progressively more responsible, taking on the obligations of the alcoholic. He feels more and more guilty; she feels more and more angry and put upon.

When the couple seeks help, the first step each must learn is essentially a compromise. John agrees to take responsibility for his drinking. Mary agrees to back off and allow John to do so.

The compromise is temporary until new and healthy behavior can replace the previous craziness. Nothing can change unless each sticks to the compromise. Easy to say, hard to do.

Neither one is initially HAPPY to make the concession in his own behavior and if one slips back into the old pattern, then that gives the other spouse a ready-made excuse to retaliate by falling back too. "John, what the heck, if you're going to drink then I am justified in acting like a shrew and treating you like a child." Or: "If you're going to nag me again, Mary, then I am justified in having a drink or two to cope with you."

To repeat: the hardest part of a compromise is to accept it and stick to my part of the bargain even if my partner slips and falls.

Another example: James is verbally abusive; Jane retaliates by withholding affection and love-making. They work out a compromise: He won't use insulting language and she will become more demonstrative. It works for a week. James slips and Jane says: "See, I knew you couldn't do it, so forget it." Or Jane declines a particular advance on his part, and James says: "I knew it. It was a ploy to get me to do what you want."

It's difficult to stick to your part of the bargain, but you do it because you like yourself and your behavior better by keeping your part of the deal. Taken at face-value, James should be happy with not being abusive, and Jane should be happy with being affectionate and enjoying sex. But when the issue becomes one of scoring points—who's right and who's wrong—then logic takes a back seat.

Well, Vince, how simple you make it sound. Yes, it is simple; BUT it is not easy. In fact, it is difficult. It sounds harsh to say it, but some can do it and some seem unable to do it. That's where therapy is supposed to help; namely to get at the underlying factors that block people from making changes in their behavior.

Expectations and *compromise,* two acquired skills that require relinquishing my own stubbornness, will lead to a more serene marriage.

13. THE FEARSOME FOURSOME #1

Criticism and Defensiveness May Lead to Divorce

Some years ago I used to conduct Pre-Cana classes, which were sessions presented by the Catholic Church to couples planning marriage. The classes were given not only to prepare couples, but also to prevent problems from arising.

However, problems do crop up after the honeymoon period. So some OJT—on the job training—helps to cope with the unforeseen. One therapist lists four bad habits that couples fall into as time goes on: **Criticism, Defensiveness, Contempt, and Withdrawal.** I call them the Fearsome Foursome of Divorce. Any one of these harmful traits will jeopardize a marriage; more than one is usually the prelude to divorce.

Criticism is a bad habit that one or both partners resort to. It is ineffective and destructive. Criticism is a severe and negative judgment about another. "How stupid it is to..." "This place looks like a pigsty..." "When are you ever going to learn..." etc.

It's so easy to fall back on a criticism. That's because it puts you on a higher moral ground. To criticize is to say that I'm better than you. I know better.

Vincent B. Cardarelli, Th.M., CADC

What can I do about it? What kind of OJT will help to avoid it? First, ask yourself whether you would say the same thing to a friend or co-worker. And if you would say it, HOW would you word it? Would you just let it all hang out? At the very least, you would think twice before you said it. The lyrics of a popular song: "You always hurt the one you love," remind us that we are less thoughtful with our spouses than we are to others.

There are, indeed, times when we need to give opinions and judgments to one another. That is, we need to be a "critic" from time to time. But we expect critics to be objective and not get carried away with their own anger and grandiosity. The phrase "constructive criticism" is sometimes used as an excuse for vituperation and venom. It is often a harsh censure rather than a critique.

You need to give and receive feedback, one to another. But if it masquerades as criticism, you weaken the bond between you. Think before you pass judgment; be thoughtful to your spouse.

Defensiveness is another destructive strategy that jeopardizes a marriage. Behavior which is taken to protect against danger or harm is defensiveness. Given our built-in "fight or flight" instinct, it is usually an impulsive reaction to defend ourselves when we are "accused" of something. We automatically defend ourselves when we perceive that we are under attack. It is an understandable response to feedback or evaluation, whether critical or not.

When it looks like your spouse has scored a point, it is an instinctive urge to strike back, to even the score; even when my partner has a legitimate complaint. It is "natural" to take it personally and become "defensive."

That response, however, leads to a tug of war. Or maybe a real battle, verbal or otherwise. Sometimes it is best not to react. That is not really "flight." It is neutral. It is strategic; it is to disengage. Don't go down the road. Don't take the bait.

When faced with criticism from your spouse, real or perceived, don't respond in kind. Let it hang there. It's like saying sticks and stones will break my bones, but names will never hurt me.

If you have to say something you can say: "I'm sorry you feel that way." Or "Let me think about that..."

I hope that it is obvious that what I have written does not apply to spousal abuse, emotional or physical. That needs to be vigorously defended against, even to the point of seeking outside help.

We can and should prepare for marriage by any means possible. But sometimes we need emotional training while we are actually "on the job."

14. THE FEARSOME FOURSOME #2

Contempt and Withdrawal Prevent Serenity and Foster Divorce

The "Fearsome Foursome" are Criticism, Defensiveness, Contempt and Withdrawal. The foursome imperils the stability of marriage.

This chapter spotlights two harmful habits: contempt and withdrawal. Similar to criticism and defensiveness, contempt and withdrawal are inappropriate expressions of irritation and anger. Instead of being more assertive and direct, a person uses a passive-aggressive style of communicating.

Contempt means to look on another with disdain and scorn. To hold in contempt is to despise; it leads to malicious ridicule and name-calling. In place of words, sometimes a look is enough: "if looks could kill, you'd be dead."

Imagine a curled lip and a cold, calculating state—like Clint Eastwood in *Dirty Harry*. Imagine the effect of aiming that at your spouse!

Wow! When one spouse shows contempt to the other, things are really bad. Not too much love or affection will follow a look or word of contempt. In fact, it just may be a prelude to an affair, or a stepping stone to divorce.

TOWARD SERENITY

The only way to correct this habit is to stop it. That's all, just stop it. Bite your tongue; count to 10; take a deep breath—whatever; but stop it.

What do you tell an older child who is reviling his younger sibling" You quietly say: Stop it! No explanation, just put limits on it. It's the same with couples; except that the limit must come from within oneself

To the credit of many couples, when they become aware of what they are doing and its effect, they stop it voluntarily. Only when you stop the contempt that can you begin to realize that you really felt hurt, or irritation, or that you disagreed with your spouse and didn't know how to express it. And that's when you resorted to disdain or sneers. If only you knew better...

Withdrawal is shown by the silent treatment, by exasperation, by sulking, by having a headache. Avoiding the issue, holding back affection, making excuses, holding a grudge. You can also withdraw by "putting on a happy face" and pretending that all is O.K., yet keeping a frosty distance.

It's like using Yoga in a perverse way. Yoga is a kind of self-hypnosis used to clear the mind, to relieve stress and produce harmony with our surroundings. Withdrawal uses the same power of self-hypnosis in a negative way, by carrying a grudge which separates us from our closest one.

My guess is that withdrawal is the most common of all "games that people play."

Those who see themselves as nice mistakenly withdraw to keep the peace. "It's wrong to be angry." I'll wait till I'm over it before I say anything." But it doesn't work—at least not in the long run.

The Fearsome Foursome—criticism, defensiveness, contempt and withdrawal—all of them are ineffective ways of communication in a marriage. When one is not heard, it is tempting to use one of these, because they do attract attention. They are effective at getting back, getting even, or confusing the issue. But they are harmful and they do not solve any problem.

Vincent B. Cardarelli, Th.M., CADC

So what do we do instead? The answer lies in learning how to use that most important (God-given) emotion—*anger*. No resolution without confrontation. That topic—how to handle anger—is the subject of the chapter on Fighting Fair.

15. PERCEPTION IS "TRUTH"

Just Because It Is True To You Doesn't Make It Right

Can you imagine Rosie O'Donnell talking to Rush Limbaugh? The last thing that you could ever expect to happen is that one would convince the other to change his/her perspective. Or that one would be persuaded to change his mind or opinion. Each one perceives the world and the people in it differently. And they're both utterly convinced that their view is the right one. Imagine if they were married!

My perception *is* the truth, the whole truth and nothing but the truth. Getting along with others depends a lot on perception, because so often one's perception IS the truth. In other words, what I perceive to be the truth IS the truth. When you say: "Well, at least that is the way it seems to me," you really mean that's the way it is.

Your perception of someone or something represents the truth for you, and you will tend to hold on tenaciously to what you believe, sometimes even in the face of overwhelming evidence to the contrary.

A husband may forget an anniversary, but while he may perceive that as a lapse, his wife may perceive it as symbolic of their whole marriage, that he doesn't care and this is just another example of it. Because of her own

Vincent B. Cardarelli, Th.M., CADC

perception, it may mean more to her than to him. Often enough, *my* perception of an event is the truth for me.

A stepson who call his step-mother "Mary" instead of "mom,' can be admired as being loyal to his real mother, or as being disrespectful to his stepmother: it depends on perception.

Perception plays an important part in our relationships with the outside world as well as in relationships. The knowledge, insight or intuition that we gain by means of our senses, forms the basis of how we perceive the world. Education, moral training and family values help as well.

Perception is the result of our "style," of our personality, and it helps us to cope with the world and with people. A rigid personality is apt to perceive a mistake by his child as an offense worthy of punishment. An easy-going personality may be less compelled to punish a child who leaves things around or a wife who is usually late.

In a marriage, if "he" is easy-going and forgets things, and "she" is meticulous and remembers all the details of the past, each one's perception of what happens between them will be different. The husband says "no big deal," and the wife says "if you loved me, you would not forget."

You can see that serenity is jeopardized by conflicting perceptions. And the reason is that for me, perception is truth. How can I possibly go against the truth? Why can't you be reasonable and see things my way?

The examples are many: husband and wife, parents and children, employer and employee, prosecutor and defense attorney, Palestinians and Israelis. By the way, that's the reason people say you should avoid the subjects of religion and politics; it's because the perceptions are so different that it usually leads to arguments.

What can two people do when each one's perception of the same event is different? If we're talking about the Giants' and Ravens' football teams, it's not such a big deal. But if the issue is a gay son in a Catholic family, or if the issue is a spouse's drinking, or if the husband is a flirt, then it's a different story. It is a big thing.

How does either side arrive at an acceptable truce when one's perception disagrees with the other's? And more importantly, how can you love the other and live serenely with one another (never mind just a truce)?

So what do you do? Can one change one's own perceptions? And if so, how do you do that?

The first step and the hardest is *not to get defensive;* not to react as if another's opinion is an attack on you. You need to intercept your instinctive reaction to "fight back." You need to skip a beat, pause, take a deep breath, count to 10, or at least 5. Easy to say, but can you do it?

If someone comes to me in the office and relates that he is using drugs, I ask him to tell me more. If, however, my own child comes to me and says the same thing, I am off the wall in a half-second. At least that is my instinctive reaction. But if I have my head on straight and am in charge of my temporary emotion, I can at least pause and ask for more information. If I don't get immediately defensive, I have some options other than flying off the handle. We won't be immediately at one another's throats.

It's not easy to sit down with your partner and say: "O.K., I'll try not to be defensive. But we're not moving until you make me understand your position. I will listen and then translate what you're saying until I can show you that I understand. I'm not going to prove that I am right. I just want to understand you."

If you say that, your partner will immediately *faint.* After she wakes up, go ahead and do exactly what you said you were going to. Pay attention. Listen—really listen.

See if you can "perceive" the event through the eyes of the other. Avoid trying to win a point. Forget about your own needs for a few minutes. Stay cool and listen. Again I say, it is not easy, and it does not come naturally. You have to work at it. "Walk a mile in the other person's moccasins."

Vincent B. Cardarelli, Th.M., CADC

A poignant example is the conflict that parents face when confronted with accepting a child who is gay. Often, he is petrified to tell his parents, because he knows that his parents believe he's committing a sin against God and nature. It goes completely against their own perception of sex and sexuality. It is difficult for the parents to listen and not judge, because it may mean that they are at risk of changing their perception.

But be careful! Becoming aware of the other's "truth" is emotionally challenging. It may cause you to change your own version of the truth, and it may further cause you to change your own beliefs and actions. The effort is worth it. It leads to mutual understanding, acceptance and serenity.

16. INTIMACY AND SERENITY #1

Intimate Knowledge Brings Serenity

For the most part, I read only novels. I borrow from the library alphabetically, and have several going at the same time.

My work for many years has been with the realities of life, and so I lean toward fiction, probably as an escape. But I also find enjoyment when the novelist departs from the narrative and uses his imagination and creativity. He will then share some personal insights, or pet peeves, or take liberty with politics, or religion or just about anything.

For example, in the novel *The Simple Truth,* David Baldacci writes this about the main character: "There is no one alive who knew him better than his wife. Maybe that was the really one important product of a successful marriage: the knowledge that there was one other soul out there who had your number, all the way down to the last decimal place."

Isn't that great? Maybe that is the attraction of marriage; namely, that you can let someone know you intimately. "Know" not in the biblical sense of having carnal knowledge of another. But "know" in the sense of being understood directly with clarity and certainty.

Vincent B. Cardarelli, Th.M., CADC

To be so familiar with another as to be without façade or disguise. Imagine! To be known by another as you really are and still be accepted and loved. Don't you think that would give you a sense of serenity?

I think that is how an affair starts. It often begins with an accidental stumbling into a shared moment of intimacy.

Sometimes in the wake of an argument with one's spouse, or a loss of a relative, or a passing period of despair, there is a need for human contact and solace. At such a time one naturally reaches out, hopefully to one's partner and spouse, or parent. But if the significant other is not there, or unaware, or unwilling to be there, then, in a vulnerable state, it's just possible that such a person will stumble into a friend, co-worker, or neighbor, who may, with the best of intentions, provide the willing ear and compassionate understanding, which is emotional intimacy.

The allure of an affair is usually not physical; or at least it does not start out that way. Friends are friends precisely because they allow you to be yourself without a façade. But since he/she is a friend, there is a universal social taboo, against the kind of intimacy that is reserved for married couples.

Yet we know that often enough, it is with a friend that one breaks the taboo. Understandably so—though not excusably so—since some intimacy already exists.

Author David Baldacci shows great insight when he writes that when someone has knowledge of me that no one else has, knows me as I am—no defenses, no dissembling—that gives me a feeling of peace and serenity. That is the kind of intimacy that we yearn for throughout life, reminiscent of the symbiotic relationship of mother and infant.

It is a gift to be so known. In fact, when God revealed himself to Moses, he called himself by the name Yahweh, or Jehovah, which means "I am Who am." Only Moses was given that intimate knowledge.

I don't know if anyone can describe what it feels like to be known as is—probably the closest experience we can have is the feeling that a fetus has of complete envelopment by the mother—safe, wrapped up, connected—no past, no future—just a real serene now. Paradise.

And "Paradise Lost" means being cast out in the world by birth, which leads to a constant seeking of the original happy condition. It's almost as if we spend the rest of our lives trying to recapture that state of bliss. And when a "true love" enters the picture, the hope and desire of being known AS I AM resurfaces, and we struggle to recreate it.

It is no surprise that we never quite succeed, that we become disillusioned and maybe tempted to seek it elsewhere.

But more about that in the next chapter.

17. INTIMACY AND SERENITY #2

There Aren't Any Shortcuts

The search for intimacy—to know and be known by another—is built into our humanity. Much of life is spent in seeking: seeking to feel better, seeking to avoid pain, seeking to find the ideal partner.

Our society puts a premium on a "relationship" as the means to be happy. The importance of a relationship ends up putting a lot pressure on the other partner to provide what one doesn't have in himself.

There is a compelling need to seek fulfillment in another. The topic of relationship is the focus of almost all magazines on the newsstand: parent and child, child and parent, men and women, adolescent and peers, boss and employee, etc. I guess it is a popular topic because it is so important, or at least we perceive it to be important.

When the relationship does not live up to my expectations, when I don't get the "high" from being with my partner, I am then tempted to seek a substitute, to seek what I need in another way.

Recently, our culture has turned more and more to drugs—prescribed or illegal - as a way to "get high," as a way to reach a "feel good state of being." For much of human history, we've searched for ways to alter the state of consciousness (to feel good.) Whether it has been to forget our harsh surroundings, come to grips with our mortality, alter a mood, explore feelings, promote social interaction escape boredom, treat a mental illness, stimulate creativity, improve physical performance or enhance the senses—no matter what—we are sorely tempted to make it better ASAP.

There are many acceptable and healthy ways to do that: "We can seek religious experiences; we can drive the body past its physical limits; we can immerse ourselves in work; we can fall in love; we can create works of art or we can read a book, see a movie, or dance until our spines tingle," (from *Uppers, Downers, and All Arounders.)* These are all ways which can help us to create a happier more serene state of being—get high.

But it is also a fact that for centuries, culture after culture has substituted psychoactive drugs as a shortcut to happiness, to getting high. A hieroglyphic from 1500 B.C. warns about using alcohol to achieve happiness.

All *substitute* behaviors such as addictions have one thing in common: to seek a high, a climax, an altered state of consciousness, whether it is in the seventh heaven of St. Teresa, or the bliss of Timothy Leary. Some of these are ego-syntonic, i.e. beneficial, and some are ego-dystonic, i.e. harmful.

If a person repeats the substitute behavior over and over, it becomes an addiction, which means getting stuck, as on a merry-go-round. Since all addictions are substitutes for the real thing, in the end they are not satisfying.

But back to intimacy. Being intimate with another—to know and be known as I am—leads to an altered state of consciousness—i.e. feeling good. This is symbolized by the act of love—'reaching a climax.'

The trouble is that you can't get intimacy out of a bottle or a pill. "Wait a minute!" you say. How about Viagra? Well, admittedly, it will give a man a renewed sense of pride and confidence, but that it will produce intimacy is doubtful.

Vincent B. Cardarelli, Th.M., CADC

Besides, who will help women to desire the newly potent man?

No, there is no substitute for intimacy, and no chemical that will provide a shortcut to the serenity that only intimacy can give to a relationship.

18. INTIMACY AND SERENITY #3

Lack of Intimacy Invites the Thief: The Affair

The intimate knowledge of another and to be known intimately by another contributes to one's serenity. Drugs and alcohol are no substitute for intimacy.

However, often enough an "affair" is used to substitute for the intimacy that one craves in a relationship. When one or both partners in a marriage feel bereft, that is, lacking in closeness, each one is vulnerable to affection from the outside.

An affair is different from a temptation, or from flirting, say at a dance or social event. Although an insecure person can see his or her partner flirting and react the same as if it were an affair, that is not what these words are about. By "affair" is meant some external, usually secretive, show of affection which the normal person will see as a violation of marital rights.

There are affairs and there are affairs. A useful distinction is that there are three kinds. The first is the "fling," the one where a partner has a short, discreet contact. It may happen at a conference, under the influence of a night of binging. It presents no real threat to the marriage. It has no "message" nor is it a substitute for intimacy. At best, it can be called a "lapse." (Henry Hyde, don't get me wrong, I am not condoning it.)

The second kind may be called "a cry for help." Such a liaison is a substitute for the real thing. It's like a thief who sneaks in almost unaware. The partner who gets involved didn't set out to pick another lover. Such an affair is *pseudo-intimate,* because it stirs up emotions which had lain dormant in the marriage. But it is not the real thing. It is brought into the relationship, and is "found out." It creates a crisis, it shakes up what had been a stagnant marriage. The offended partner has to pay attention: and in that sense it is a cry for help, albeit inappropriate.

This is the kind that I see most of the time in counseling. And if the couple comes and stays in counseling for a period of time, the marriage survives by making the necessary changes in BOTH partners. It becomes a more intimate relationship. The affair was used as a "wake up call."

The third kind, not frequent, is an exit visa, a way out of the marriage. It is a serious threat to the marriage. The original intimacy was lost or was never there in the first place. The husband and wife have reached a point of no return, for whatever reason, and counseling will not help save the marriage, although it may keep them from severe conflict.

Several periods in the marriage are more likely to "invite' the thief into the space between husband and wife. One is early on, when commitment has not been established. Another is around the birth of children, or when the children leave home. And still another likely time is when a husband or wife becomes aware that his/her partner has withdrawn and won't fight back, or won't share feelings, i.e. avoids intimacy.

When a couple does have recourse to counseling, one of the necessary topics to discuss is, *what is the meaning of the affair?* If the affair is a substitute, then it is important for the couple to realize what happened to *both* of them prior to the affair; what led up to the affair, and what each contributed to the possibility of this happening. And next they must decide what is going to happen now that there has been disclosure.

No doubt that the person who strayed is responsible for his/her behavior. But both must accept some responsibility for the process that follows disclosure. There's usually a great need to "talk to somebody." If you pick friends, know that they will be on your side, and not necessarily give good advice. In fact, advice is not what is needed. What is needed is a non-judgmental atmosphere in which there is a no-win goal: nobody wins, otherwise everybody loses.

Pick somebody who knows what he is doing. It's too soon for a lawyer, but not too late for a therapist. The essential question for the couple is: Is this the end of our relationship, or is it the beginning of a new one? Both will eventually have to make some changes. Strong efforts are needed by the couple; no fooling around. They need to make a commitment to the work of reconciliation. And then the next question is how do we ensure that we put intimacy back into our life together to prevent the "thief" from sneaking in again.

19. LOVE, SEX AND SERENITY

Learning to Curb Your Sexual Appetite Helps Define Love

The movie *High Fidelity* starred John Cusack and Iben Hjejle, both of whom are real naturals as actors. It's about a man, Rob, who runs a record store, and on the side, keeps thousands of his own records in his littered apartment. He spends his time sorting through the records and arranging them in all kinds of order—alphabetical, chronological, etc.

Rob and Laura (Hjejle) are going through a break-up, and that prompts Rob to begin another list, entitled *My Five All-Time Greatest Break-ups.* He does the same thing with his girlfriends that he does with his records. The movie shows in flashback what happened in other relationships. In the meantime, Laura is in the process of moving out of the apartment, and Rob tries to figure out why this keeps happening to him.

Marshal Fine, critic for the Gannett News Service, reviewed the movie and has some lines worth repeating. "Rob is an arrested juvenile in the body of an adult,' he writes. But when Laura moves out to live with another man, Rob is determined to win her back—but isn't sure why.

"It's not that Rob is a bad guy—just a distracted one," according to Fine. "Relationships to him are like new CD's; greatly anticipated, initially devoured, then gradually put aside when something new comes along. He's sincere... (but) his notions about romance have been formed by the albums and songs he loves."

And listen to another wonderful insight by Mr. Fine: "As anyone with a little time in the trenches can tell you, romantic love is something you read about, watch in movies or hear about in the lyrics of songs. As Rob slowly discovers, the true definition of love is learning to put aside that urge for something new. It's also about developing new levels in the relationship you have, once that shiny layer of newness has worn off."

I've read that quotation numerous times, and I am envious that Mr. Fine is able to put such words together. I see that "urge for something new" repeated over and over in the couples that come for therapy. In fact, I see it in myself and in the world around me.

Growing slowly bored with the commonplace, the soul begins to yearn for something new—and dangerously, *someone* new.

The movie is also a statement about young men of today. I don't know whether it is a fear of commitment, or whether it the lure of the rush that one gets from the promise of a new sexual experience. Kind of like a new Playboy magazine each month, with its promise of someone new—a new playmate.

In the film, when Rob talks to the audience (in voice-over, with the camera recording the action), he explains himself in detail. As he does so, he wins the audience over. While watching him, I was reminded of the many people who have affairs and "explain" how it happened in the hopes that it will redeem them. "If only you knew the whole story..." Rob, like many philanderers, is earnest and likeable, he is a guy who understands his own mistakes—and then goes out and repeats them all over again.

He can go from despondency to sexual arousal in the space of a phone call. What he does with sex, others do with sweets or alcohol. It's like looking at a lonely Saturday night, and having a phone call come in to invite you to a party. All of a sudden things look up.

At the end of the movie, Rob begins to figure out that Laura is the girlfriend he wants, and he does not want to lose her.

Fine says of Rob's character: "Cusack has exactly the right blend of excitability, dread and wit to make Rob a multifaceted and ingratiating figure, a fellow you like even as you recognize his shortcomings. You root for him to see what is obvious to all around him; that love is about the long haul, rather than the initial rush."

Ah, yes. There are many teachers out there to instruct us about love and what it is and is not. But like Rob, when the pupil is ready, the teacher appears. It seems that to arrive at an understanding of the balanced connection between love and sex, we learn as much—and maybe more—from our own mistakes as from the lessons that parents, clergy and therapists teach us.

20. SEX ALONE DOES NOT SUSTAIN A RELATIONSHIP

Before the sexual revolution of the '60's, couples had to decide whether or not to have sex (meaning intercourse) before marriage.

In the 90's, couples have to decide whether or not to have sex (score!) on the first date.

Growing up before that hectic time, kids hardly even heard or said the "f" word. But in the movie "Goodfellas", the "f" word was used 296 times.

Things are different. And that is an understatement.

Americans today are oversexualized. Maybe it is more accurate to say *over-genitalized.* Even the word "sex," which is a word that could mean everything from talking intimately, to touching, to kissing or to the meaning it has today: intercourse. The word "sex" is used almost exclusively to mean penetration and climax.

Good "sex" makes us feel better, makes our relationship work, solves problems. This is what we have come to believe. Sex, or the promise of it, sells everything from lacy underwear to footballs, body products to automobiles.

MAXIM, a magazine for men, features an article entitled "30 New Sex Tricks." The other articles are decorated with nubile women who seem to promise a few tricks of their own. (I subscribe, but only to read the articles, of course.)

If it is true that sex produces true intimacy, then how come couples, married or not, get bored with "sex" and seek new partners every few years?

"We've lost sight of the element of a relationship that's truly gratifying, and that is intimacy: an open, emotional exchange...in which mutuality, respect and assertion go back and forth," says Dr. Drew Pinsky.

The 60's generation—the hippies, flower people, and even many religious leaders—rebelled against a history of repression. Their aim was to throw off the shackles of sin and condemnation, and create instead a world that was more open and accepting.

But young people today have not had to do that; they have not had to repress themselves. Children today are not told: "Say the Rosary when you get bad thoughts." On the contrary, sex education starts in grammar school, often as young as age 6. Parents and children are encouraged to talk about "Sex."

But if "Sex" Education means "Genital" Education—how to use them and get the most out of them—then we miss the opportunity of teaching our children about intimacy—**real** intimacy.

Elsewhere in this book I write on the topic of intimacy, and defined it as the ability to know and be known by another. In the Bible, "to know someone" meant to have sex with that person. *"And Adam knew Eve his wife, and she conceived."* (Gen.4:1)

But for today's couple to know one another, it is not enough to have sex with that person. People need to learn the concept of mutuality and the ways of attaining it.

Women (and men) who ask "Is that all he (she) wants from me?" are really saying "I need more than sex." Prostitutes (I've heard) usually don't kiss their johns, because kissing is too intimate.

What people need is a kind of intimacy that is mutual; a way of communicating that is verbal, thoughtful and respectful. Couples need to give and receive affection in ways other than the sex act.

We need a definition of 'sex" that encompasses more than just "f—" which was the point, I think, of the movie *Eyes Wide Shut*. Sex is continually gratifying, but only when it includes more than just the physical and mechanical act. The sex act by itself does not sustain a relationship.

It is sad to see that our capacity for intimacy has not reached its potential. Abusive and dysfunctional families diminish the capacity of their children to take the risk of real emotional contact. So also for children of families that are *busy, busy, busy*—always running and "doing" things, rather than "being."

We become *human doings* rather than *human beings*. And so, one of things that we must "do" well is have sex, and if we don't, then we wrongly conclude that something is terribly wrong with the relationship.

One woman told me she went out on a first date, and when the man was unable to become fully tumescent, she was "destroyed" and refused to date him again. He could easily have been insecure, or feeling guilty. But since she didn't know anything else beside his inability to perform, she quickly concluded that he was the wrong guy for her.

Serenity comes from emphasizing real intimacy, instead of stressing only the sexual aspect of it. Real intimacy has many aspects to it and needs to be assessed in ways other than genitally.

21. THE JOYS OF FRIENDSHIP

Someone has said that you're wealthy if you have good friends and good health. Of course, there are those who also say that if you have enough money, you buy both. But there is no doubt about it—friendship is really a joy, and as such adds to serenity.

As I have grown older, it has become more important to me to reconnect with my friends of years ago. Some have moved away, some are nearby, and some are unreachable. No matter. Some years ago, I looked up several of the friends I had growing up in Raritan and Somerville, my home area. Since then I made it my business to keep in touch, one way or another.

When my daughter got married recently, I invited them to come and join the festivities. They came and all sat together. It was truly a joy to be in their midst.

Sam Keen, author of *To Love and Be Loved,* says: "It is because friendship contains the largest quantity of enjoyment that it is the most stable and enduring of all the modes of love." He goes on to say: "Friendship demands no romantic frenzy, no howling at the moon. It depends on nothing so stout as obligation, as fragile as a pretty face, or as irrational as the thick sinews of blood and clan. It depends only on mutual delight."

I have seen numerous couples in my counseling practice who were passionately entangled. But it did not seem that they *enjoyed* one another. Friendship seemed to be missing in their togetherness.

I spent more than 15 years in the clergy. I respected and admired hundreds of men and women; and numerous people respected and admired me. But only a few have remained as *friends.* Respect and admiration are indeed forms of love, but are not as enjoyable as friendship- and not as lasting.

Friendship is not conditional. It just *is.* Sancho Panches, side-kick of Don Quixote, *The Man of La Mancha*, was asked by Dulcinea: "Why do you stay with him, seeing all the trouble he causes you?" He answers: "Because I *like* him." No conditions. To enjoy one another is enough.

S/he is my friend not because of what I can get out of it. It is not because I am a star and he is my satellite; or vice-versa. It is not because my friend introduces me to famous people, or enables me to go places I never would otherwise have seen. It is not because I can gain entry to golf courses, or get front row seats at the theatre. It is just because he is he, and I am I.

Friendship is liberating, it allows you to be yourself. It is not, by contrast, possessive and clinging. It does not prohibit or prevent. If, for example, you are afraid to tell your friend how you feel, or what you have done, for fear of hurting her, or making her angry, then you have to wonder how much of a friend s/he really is.

Our relationship does not trigger competition. I don't want to have more money than he, or have more influence than he. I bask in his success, and he in mine.

If my friend gives a talk on how to do therapy, I sit in the audience and revel in his success. But if a professional acquaintance gives a talk, I am quick to "critique" and find flaws in his theories and techniques.

There is no jealousy in friendship, such as you find in lovers. If my friend is of the opposite sex, I don't horn in

Vincent B. Cardarelli, Th.M., CADC

when another man is talking to her; or try to tell a better story so as to look good in her eyes. It is difficult for a married person to allow his/her spouse to have a friend of the opposite sex.

I don't ask: "Am I a better friend than _____?" Whatever I get from my friend is enough to last until the next time. And if a lot of time elapses between visits, when we finally get together, it is as if no time has passed. I do not begrudge the fact that he did not call on my birthday (but he usually remembers anyway.)

"I" am the one who receives, and I know that my friend feels the same way. Keen says that between lovers who are friends, "pleasure is a Ping-Pong ball that gets batted back and forth."

In a different vein, it is difficult for parents to trust their children to pick their own friends, and not to do it for them—especially when their choices are not like "us." If parents and children have developed their *own* friendship, then they will trust one another to learn for themselves which are the real friends (and will last) and which are not (and will be transient.)

Everyone agrees that it is the job of parents to monitor their children's friends. But the way they will influence their children's choice is not by stringent rules backed by punishment, but by a judicious repetition of their own values and attitudes.

It is a great gift to give—that of enjoying your friend, in simple pleasure; and it is a great gift to receive—enjoying a friend in return.

They say you pick your friends, but you don't pick your family. Still and all, it would be a joy to have as your friends—your spouse, your parents, and your children. Then you would *like* them as well as *love* them.

> *Love to faults is always blind.*
> *Always is to joy inclined,*
> *Lawless, winged and unconfined,*
> *And breaks the chains from every mind.* Wm Blake

Section III—Parents and Children

1. IMPRINTING #1

We inherit more than just our looks

The scientist, Gregor Mendel, showed that a child inherits discrete "particles" from his parents, which are called *genes*. Various combinations of genes make up the individuality of the newborn child. Though different from parents, the child has some biologically determined characteristics similar to the parents: "Gee, he looks like his mom (dad)."

Just as we inherit physical traits, we inherit behavioral traits as well; that's called attachment theory or *imprinting*. Behavioral scientists define attachment as an infant's comfortable sense of trust in its mother. The process of attachment takes place when two factors are present: 1) the proximity of a safe adult, usually the mother; and 2) secure caretaking behavior of the adult.

"Most psychologists agree that a child's attachment to his primary caretaker (usually the mother) forms the foundation for its emotional development." (U.S.News and World Report) A secure attachment provides the basis for a healthy emotional life and a blueprint for satisfactory relationships later on. On the other hand, a weaker bond, i.e. an "insecure attachment" to the mother or caretaker, can leave the child at risk for later behavioral and emotional problems.

Like a blueprint for future behavior, the brain and the central nervous system are imprinted by the experience of attachment, whether it was secure or insecure, and later emotional and behavioral patterns are the result of such imprinting.

You will remember that this was the reasoning that the defense team used for Jesse Timendequas, dramatizing his background and using his experiences as "mitigating factors." There was, the lawyers said, "a similarity between what he did to Megan Kanka and what was done to him as a child." That was the trial that begat "Megan's Law."

You may or may not agree with that (especially when it comes to criminal behavior), but folk wisdom incorporates that reasoning in proverbs such as "like father—like son," or "The apple does not fall far from the tree." Certainly, these proverbs are not always accurate, but they do reflect the belief that faulty or incomplete learning can have later consequences. Early childhood experiences and patterns of interaction between child and parents are often predictors of future behavior, for good or for ill.

A national study has indicated that infants who attend poor quality day-care centers in the first years of their lives are "insecurely attached" to the substitute caregivers (people who take the place of mother for long periods). These infants are "at risk" for later aggressive behavior, are unable to learn, and lack compassion for others. This is especially true when the basic mother-child relationship is weak to begin with.

What I would like you to consider is that there not only are some "insecurely attached" children at our day-care centers and schools today, but also that there are as well some "insecurely attached" adults (who are the parents of those children).

Adults who have developed faulty learning patterns, tend to repeat those patterns with their own children. Adults who are now married, relate to one another with patterns of communication and interpersonal affection that are the result of insecure imprinting.

The purpose here is not to shower blame on anyone, but to shed light on the imperfection of human nature, and to emphasize the need for continued learning. We need to stop and look at the patterns we inherited and see if they are providing us what we need. If not, we would benefit from doing something new and different.

If you follow the instinct of the imprinting that you received as a child, you will repeat the patterns that you learned as an infant (yes, it can go all the way back there.)

Like a knee-jerk reaction, your behavior will be determined by pathways that the brain and central nervous system "learned" at the knee of your parents. Your actions will be prompted more by impulse than by intellect.

If you were "securely attached" then for the most part your behavior will be appropriate and productive; if you were "insecurely attached" then you may have problems with your behavior and wonder why it doesn't work; why you and your child or your spouse, are not getting along.

This chapter is the first part of three. There will follow some examples, and then some suggestions on how to offset the legacy of insecure attachment, and ineffective imprinting.

2. IMPRINTING #2

Early Care Has Huge Impact on Kids

As outlined in the first section on imprinting, the kind of security an infant develops with its primary caregiver (and to a lesser extent with secondary caregivers) provides the initial design for future behavior. What the child has learned and experienced provides a blueprint for the emotional and behavioral patterns that will be re-created with significant people in later life.

What you are reading is not about abused or neglected children, but about ordinary and moral people. Some of us have been insecurely attached in not-so-traumatic ways. So we won't be led to a life of crime or serious dysfunction. But the quality of our life may be affected, for example at home with our family; or at work with our bosses and co-workers.

"Good, early care has a huge impact on kids," writes Sue Schallenbarger. Studies have shown that good care, e.g. in Head Start, can raise IQ and performance. It is also true that good care has an impact on emotional and behavioral growth. Attachment theory has shown that interactions between child and caregiver have a lasting imprint on the child and serve as an instinctual blueprint, a kind of automatic response to certain similar situations. Thus, he will tend to repeat certain behavior with spouse, children, authority figures, etc. Equally important, the imprinting can affect how he acts in stressful or "dangerous" situations.

I'm happy that you have stayed with this chapter so long, since it has been theoretical. So let me be more concrete: I'll apply it first to one's style of life. An example is found in one of Jay McInerney's novels. He describes a 13-year old boy whose mother "spoke for him, adjusted his clothes and hair and generally treated him so much like a puppet that he seemed not to have developed any volition of his own." You can imagine an older version of this boy who has become compliant and unable to make his own decisions, first with his friends, then with his wife or take Annie, who lives with very good and religious parents, who themselves have many *shoulds* and *oughts,* and train Annie the same way. She may have trouble with guilt even into her adult life. She may very well be unable to say "no" to her parents, and avoid even legitimate pleasures, and sprinkle her speech with "I'm sorry..."

A common example is adolescent onset of anxiety. The genesis of anxiety occurs when the caretaking adult is unpredictable (e.g. disappears in the aisle of ShopRite). Or maybe the parent is violent, or fails to provide a safe environment. The child manifests "searching" behavior, becomes unsettled and screeches (anxiety). When the caretaker returns the child hangs on—clinging behavior. Clinging behavior then reappears in the adolescent years.

If the young child experiences repeated anxiety, then later on, when stressful situations occur, or when a relationship is threatened, like the break-up of a "steady boy/girlfriend", the knee-jerk reaction may be a replay of the 'imprinted" behavior: unsettled, crying, clinging. Anxiety can reach the level of "too much stress," or panic, or obsessive ruminations.

Still another example deals with intimate behavior. Some people are comfortable with hugs; some cringe from effusive shows of affection. Some people have trouble with secondary impotence. Although there may be other reasons for dysfunction with intimacy (some serious reasons, too), it would be well to look to "insecure imprinting" as a factor (which is not so serious.)

A final example is style of communication. Certain words, certain topics, certain ways of acting can lead to arguments and long destructive silences between couples. Ask yourselves: When you talk to one another in this way, whom—or what—does it remind you of?

Examine your past without blaming anyone. It may throw some light on your present behavior. When we can become aware of what we are doing, then we can change it and do it right. The next chapter will make suggestions on how to do that.

3. IMPRINTING #3

Be Proactive: Drive Your Own Bus

This chapter, the third in a series, continues to show how early child care can impact on emotional and behavioral growth.

Through insecure attachment, or incomplete learning, we may develop some unhealthy patterns of reacting. These patterns are usually instinctual and not thought-out. The good news is that it's possible to interrupt and derail those annoying knee-jerk reactions which get us into trouble.

If you have a suspicion that a recurring behavior is a remnant of faulty early child-care and/or learning, you may need therapy. But before you go that route, there may be something that you can do about it yourself.

As a child, Michael was always told how wonderful he was. "To-be-the-best" became a need and then grew to be a compulsion. So when people told him to ease up, or to be satisfied with what he had, he got irritated and angry.

Winning, being first, was the only goal. Waiting in line, listening while another expressed an opinion, following instructions—all that grated on his nerves, and he reacted with hostility and impatience.

As he grew older, he realized that he was reacting instinctively that he had "an attitude," and as a result he made an effort to look at himself in a different light.

He learned to say to himself: "So what if I'm not a CEO at 34. Or a Tiger Woods or a John Travolta? I can do a lot of things, maybe not expertly, but enough to hold my own. I'm O.K. the way I am, and don't have to win in everything to prove my worth."

You too may find an area of your life that repeatedly gives you trouble. You may find yourself bristling at a situation—like driving your car. You may feel that you deserve a lot better than you have been given. You may avoid situations where you will be in the limelight.

You may get the same kind of negative feedback from time to time. For example, a woman relates that her ex-sometimes told her that she "shut down" when they were discussing something important. Her new boyfriend told her the same thing. In another example, a codependent husband was told by his wife that she has to guess at what he wants.

If you are faced with impulsive, repetitive behavior—don't ask *Why?* Rather ask yourself, "O.K. what can I do about it? How can I short-circuit the old behavior and learn a new one?"

The first step is to **BECOME AWARE**. Get beyond the first line of defense. Become aware of that surging bile that starts in your stomach and erupts in harsh words; of the desire to defend yourself against perceived insults; of the urge to solve someone else's problem; of the need to win an argument.

"AHA! — There it is again!" Now you have identified the virus in the system. Now you are aware of when the "child"—the faulty imprinting—takes over.

Michael's script of being the best came from a loving family. He had to be top of his class, win the prize at a talent show, etc. Later on, he was able to recognize the automatic urge in him. Until he was aware, he couldn't do much about the automatic response.

Your early script, or imprinting, may have given you messages that linger still. You may have learned to take care of others first, or take care of yourself first (and seemed selfish), or you may have inherited a temper, or impulsive tendencies of a different kind. Maybe your family did not tolerate mistakes, and so you learned to lie or dissemble to cover them up. Sex may have been dirty. You may have had to resort to whining to get what you wanted.

No matter. Train yourself, first, to recognize that reactive impulse—that knee-jerk reaction.

Step two is **SKIP A BEAT**. As soon as you notice the spontaneous urge is about to take over, stop. Just stop. SKIP A BEAT. Refuse to go down the pathway prompted by your instinct. To control the habit, take a deep breath; say "Well, now, let's see. I'm not sure what I feel right now, but give me a minute."

Pause. Look before you leap. Put your brain in gear before you engage your tongue.

Once Michael was able to skip a beat, he was then free to pick a different option. When you stop for a moment, you cut the wire to your hot button. That is what one man learned when he skipped a beat; his wife told him that he seemed to be listening to her more. By the way, how many times have you heard that before "You're just not listening."

Step three is to **CHOOSE NEW BEHAVIOR**. Take your time and ask what you want to do right now. What do I want to say? Do I need to react at all? What would I tell someone else to do in this situation?

Experiment with different responses. The ability to make this kind of a choice applies especially to discipline of children. It applies, also, to heated discussions when someone "pushes your buttons."

Step three requires perceptual restructuring—that is, looking at something in a different way. What's the difference if I get there 3 ½ minutes later? My boss may look like a tyrant, but he is really insecure down deep. It's also called "thinking outside the box."

Michael adopted the phrase "Jack of all trades, master of none." He was then more comfortable with a lower spot on the totem pole.

Step four is **DRIVE YOUR OWN BUS.** As an adult, your life is more manageable and serene if you are in charge of your behavior. If some inherited trait rules your reactions before you can think about it and are able to act responsibly, you are not in charge. If someone pushes your buttons and you react without thinking, you're like a puppet, and you are not *driving your own bus.*

When you stop, and put your mind to it, you can experiment with new behavior. You are then in charge. I'm not saying that you need to do this in every situation. If you did that you'd look like a local bus, stuttering along and stopping at every station.

Most of the time, your training, your education and your 'imprinting" will serve you well as you respond to life and it's new and variegated events. But sometimes you will hear a voice say: "Oh, Oh, I've been here before." It's then that your serenity depends on driving your own bus.

4. THE LOSS OF INNOCENCE

Judith Viorst has written a best-seller entitled *Necessary Losses.* Her point is that life is filled with losses, and some of them are *necessary,* that is, they cannot be avoided.

Each person passes the various stages of life: innocence (childhood) to adolescence (transition) to adulthood (maturity). The passage from one to the other involves a "loss" of some kind. This chapter deals with the 'loss of innocence.'

For a child to grow into an adolescent, he/she needs to "lose his innocence." Some people call that experiencing the realities of life. For some it is a rude awakening, a shock to find out the "truth" of life. That awakening can be as benign as learning that there is no Santa Claus. Or it can be as jolting as finding out that one is adopted.

Eric Erikson taught that the first stage of life is when the infant/child has to balance out "basic trust versus basic distrust." It is during this stage that the child needs to learn how to trust and hope in the outside world. It is the job of the child to acquire a sense of confidence and ease with the outside world, mainly his parents, but also with others and with experiences. As he reaches out, hopefully he experiences under the tutelage of his parents, that the world is not evil or dangerous, and so he ventures out "innocently."

Vincent B. Cardarelli, Th.M., CADC

If he doesn't experience that innocence, if his job is imperfectly done, if instead he feels that the world is dangerous, then he stands the chance of being insecure, anxious or depressed, which may carry throughout life.

The parents' job is to guide by both permission and prohibition, in such a way as to convey to the child a deep conviction that there is a meaning to what they and the child are doing. "Trust me and follow me," say the parents.

An "innocent" person is one who is like a child, i.e., without sin or malice. Innocence implies being guileless, naïve, inexperienced, unsophisticated and trusting. Some people are able to maintain innocence throughout life. My mother was an example of this. She was always described as an innocent person, and as a result saw no evil in anyone else. That her son could make a mistake or do something less than good was inconceivable to her. When she finally saw him as imperfect, capable of making a mistake, she "lost her innocence." She became depressed, and began to question other beliefs. Many people, like Peter Pan, prolong the innocent phase of life.

The loss of innocence is when the trust instilled in childhood is challenged. The growing child has a rude awakening that all is not Camelot, and is thrown back on his own resources. One's relationship with others and with the outside world is tested and possibly shaken. Now the basic trust and distrust rises again, and the developing personality needs to act on his own—i.e. in a responsible manner.

One loses his virginal, unviolated view of the world as made up of only good; one now one sees it as it is—imperfect, sometimes dangerous, and (alas!) recognizes that he/she is indeed a part of that imperfect world.

If the loss of innocence happens too early, as in families where parents are distant, untrustworthy or abusive, then the child becomes neurotic and carries that ambivalence of anxiety or depression into adolescence and/or adulthood.

Loss of innocence usually happens in early adolescence. It is then, says Erikson, that we "develop the prerequisites in physiological growth, mental maturation and social responsibility to experience and pass through the crisis of identity."

Some, like my mother, can maintain innocence till later. Others, "like the fictional Peter Pan, decide that they won't become 'grown up,' opting instead to remain a permanent boy." (Viorst)

However, normal development demands that we lose our innocence, and there is a natural resistance to that change, and facing that change presents a hard choice:

> I'd rather suffer
> Every unspeakable suffering God sends,
> Knowing it was I that suffered,
> I that earned the need to suffer,
> I that acted, I that chose,
> Than wash my hands with yours in that
> Defiling innocence. Can we be men
> And make an irresponsible ignorance
> Responsible for everything?
> (J.B., by A. MacLeish)

"The answer to that question (says Judith Viorst)—the grownup's only answer to that question—has to be **NO**...There comes a time when we aren't allowed **NOT TO KNOW**." Somewhere along the way we must recognize childhood's end—and we must decide to grow up.

That is called the 'loss of innocence' and with it comes responsibility and serenity.

5. PROLONGED ADOLESCENCE

The period or stage of innocence normally melds into the adolescent stage, when one's identity begins to be formed as much by the realities of life as it had been by the imprinting of early development. One of the tasks of adolescence is to grow from the dependence of childhood into the independence of a responsible adult.

I think my generation, coming of age in the 40's, was the last that went from childhood right into adulthood. Those before me went into service and some, in their early 20's, became non-commissioned officers leading squadrons of men into battle. When they came home, they got married and had no "transition" into adulthood. If they didn't go into service, they got a job and accepted the responsibility of their own lives.

The point is that prior to 1940, there was no "adolescence." You went from being dependent to being responsible. The transitional period of adolescence was "created" after WW II. It was identified as between the years of 14 and 18. As time went on, that phase was extended to 22, the age when dependent children graduated from college, and were considered adults.

But in the 80's, social, cultural and economic changes occurred which delayed responsible adulthood even more. Many go on to further study, not able to support themselves until ages 26 or later. Some adult children are still at home in their 20's, and others return home after failing at marriages or at the ability to support themselves.

Still others, because of circumstances sometimes beyond their intentional control, will find themselves married too soon, or burdened with financial debt caused by some impulsive and "adolescent" impulse.

Further, a significant number of adult children have attained chronological maturity, but have postponed emotional maturity because of misuse of alcohol and/or drugs. Anyway, there are many adults between the ages of 20 and 30 who in a variety of ways have *prolonged* their adolescence.

Adolescence is a period of time when the child develops into an adult. Different cultures assign different ages, and use different rituals, to identify that period. However, all seem to agree that two tasks need to be completed in order to attain adulthood: one is physical maturity, meaning that secondary sexual characteristics unfold and ripen; and second is emotional maturity, meaning responsibility and accountability are achieved.

Physical maturity usually blossoms during the teen years, so that most 18 year-olds have developed to their full potential. It is expected that emotional maturity occur at the same time, namely during adolescence. However, it seems that emotional adulthood is frequently postponed until the early twenties, or even later, such as during the first marriage. (And sometimes, sadly, even *after* the first marriage.)

The 90's have also spawned a number of adult children who have moved back home with their parents, after having been on their own for awhile. Add these to the substance abusers, and what you end up with is a lot of adults who have prolonged their own adolescence who are now *parents* of adolescents. It's like the blind leading the blind.

One of the symptoms of prolonged adolescence is an avoidance (fear) of responsibility. Avoiding responsibility is manifested in not taking ownership of one's actions. For example, in marriage, one spouse says: "WE don't communicate." How much harder it is to take ownership by saying: "I don't communicate." It is the fear of responsibility that makes someone rationalize and defend his action. "I did it because...etc." The reason I goofed is outside of myself—it's not me.

Blaming others is another way of saying the same thing. You have heard children say: "It is all YOUR fault," when something goes amiss. An adult needs to hold himself accountable for both the good and the bad of what happens.

To become responsible, learn to say "I" more often, i.e., to own your feelings, opinions and actions. Avoid seeking solutions outside of yourself, by blaming others. Start with yourself and make changes there first.

Another symptom of Prolonged Adolescence is impulsive behavior, i.e., the desire for the "quick fix." Impulsiveness is seen in adolescent behavior when one seeks out the "perfect high," goes anywhere, buys anything, uses anything either to forget, or to cope, or to relieve stress.

Impulsive behavior is reflected in a person's inability to postpone gratification. It is understandable for a child... "King Baby"...to demand of his parents: "I want it and I want it NOW!." But it is prolonged adolescence for an adult to do the same, or for an adult to be impatient with his child for not getting what he—the parent—wants.

You'll see an adult who has prolonged his growing up, impatient at the wheel of his car, or in line at the market, or at school meetings berating the teacher.

To work diligently toward a goal, to be patient with interruptions, to remain serene when you don't get your own way, to postpone gratification, <u>these</u> are signs of adulthood and maturity.

We are all imperfect and will make mistakes. But imperfection is different from prolonged adolescence. A sense of responsibility and a general patience with life are signs of growing up.

6. THE FAMILY #1

The Newly-Defined Family

It is obvious that the family contributes mightily to the serenity of its members. So let's look at the family and see how it is evolving and what would be a good definition of "family" for today's world. Then in the next chapter we'll discuss what a "good" family is.

Many recent articles have reported how the nature of the American family is changing drastically and is poised to change even more dramatically in the coming century. For example, one newspaper wrote that a majority of people with children today are raising them in a different kind of family than the one in which they were raised.

The same article summarizes a survey, called *The Emerging 21st Century American Family,* with the following:

- By 1998, only 56 percent of adults were married, compared with nearly 75 percent in 1972.
- Because of high divorce rates, cohabitation and single parenthood, a majority of families rearing children in the next century probably will not include the children's original two parents. In 1998, only 51 percent lived in a two-parent family.

- The percentage of U.S. households composed of married couples with children dropped from 45 percent in 1970 to 26 percent in 1998.
- Children living with single parents increased from less than one in 20 in 1972 to almost one in 5 in 1998, while the percentage of children living in a blended household more than doubled, from 3.8 percent to 8.6 percent.
- The number of households with unmarried adults and no children more than doubled to 33 percent, becoming the nation's *most common* arrangement.

And the experts say that the trend will continue. Here are some predictions (from the same article):

- By 2006, eight times as many children 12-17 will be living with 55- to 64-year olds than today.
- More than 8 million baby boomers already are grandparents. Of that number, 28 percent have children from their later marriages who are almost the same age as their grandchildren.
- 32 million baby boomers will be grandparents by 2007, and they will do things that used to be done by parents, such as travel.

To repeat: This chapter aims to define what a family is. Obviously, we need to define it a little differently than we used to. We can't say that a family is two biological parents with 2.8 norm of biological children, living in the same house.

The first characteristic of a *family* is that two or more people are living together, usually under one roof and taking their place as a unit of society. When you get a number of "units" together, you then have a town, or a city, etc.

It's important to distinguish a family from a household. Two men sharing the rent of an apartment, or some similar opportune arrangement do not qualify as a "family."

In a modern definition of family, rather than listing *who* constitutes a family (for example, parents children, stepparents, single parents, etc.) I think we must list *what* makes up a family. So to that end, I suggest that there are four characteristics necessary to identify the people living together as a family: **parenting, training, community and haven.**

- **Parenting.** We have been used to seeing "parents," i.e. mother and father, either biological or step, providing the nurturing for children. But when there are children in the grouping, others can provide this need for the young. The role of parenting can be assumed by grandparents, Dutch uncles, etc. What is needed in a family is a real person—parent, guarantor, mentor, relative—who provides the love and acceptance needed by the developing children
- **Training.** There need to be rules to live by: different in different places and countries. But rules nonetheless. Society and culture require acceptable behavior. Parents usually provide such training, but it can also be provided by groups, such as kibbutz, religious orders or schools, or communes. Training is sometimes called discipline.
- **Community.** A family needs to have activities which draw the members together. Thus dinners, anniversaries, traditions both cultural and religious, all these provide for the need to be "together." So you can have various kinds of families—biological, cultural, recreational, prayerful, etc. Community provides for the social need of "belonging." Belonging to a group provides the background for the separation process needed to become an adult.

- **Haven.** No matter what happens to you—young or old—you can always return to your family and be accepted. At least that is the ideal and it is the meaning of the parable of the prodigal son. You remember the emphasis on "roots" and what it means in terms of knowing oneself.

These four elements, in my opinion, are what describe the notion of "family," and if they are present in any of the new configurations of people living together, then the word family applies.

As you read this, what is your reaction and opinion? How do you define family?

I suggest you bring up the subject with your own family, and ask such questions as: What is the meaning of family? How many different variations of family can you identify? What does it mean to you to belong to *this* family?

As for the question what is the relationship between family and serenity: that will be discussed in the next chapter.

7. THE FAMILY #2

The Family and Serenity

A good family guarantees serenity and also guarantees good children. Who would argue with that statement? It is usually accepted as a truism. But is it always true?

The question is: What is a *good family?* Does a good family always have good children? Can bad children come from a good family? Or good children from a bad family?

Usually people answer these questions by looking at the idea of "nature vs. nurture." Some will say the answer is what a child receives in his genetic tape, his *nature;* others (a la Freud) will base their answer on how a child has been raised, his quality of *nurturing.* What causes good or bad children? Is it: "That's what he was born with" or "Give me the child for the first 5 years, and I will show you the man."

And now to add to the discussion, comes a book *The Nurturing Assumption,* which says that parents have little power to determine the sort of people their children will become. "It is what the children experience outside the home, in the company of their peers, that matters most. Parents don't socialize children; children socialize children," the book says.

Vincent B. Cardarelli, Th.M., CADC

Well, whatever reasons you give to explain the behavior of both children and adults, one thing that we can agree on is that the family will affect one's serenity. How you feel about yourself, your attitude, your world view and your sense of being effective in the world, will depend in great part on the family experience you had growing up.

So it's important to know what it is that makes a family "good." What do people mean when they say that? When I asked my son-in-law that question, he said: "At least in educational circles, I think they would call a family good if the children are well-behaved. And if the children are bad, then they would conclude that it must be a "bad" family."

According to some, if the children have behavioral problems, then we judge the family as being bad, or dysfunctional (the buzz word.) Uh-huh. What do you think? Can bad children come from good families? Or, on the contrary, can good children come from bad families? Or can good children only come from good families? Is it the parents' fault if the children get into trouble? Is it the moral quality of a family that determines the behavior of the members of the family?

There's got to be a better way of looking at families other than bad and good. Maybe we shouldn't even ask about *good or bad.* Maybe a question like: Does this family, no matter what it looks like, provide for the needs of **everyone** involved—adults and children. What makes a family a *family?*

A true family fulfills four needs for everyone in it: **Parenting, Training, Community and Haven.** In such a family, each member both gives and gets—gives what is needed to the other and gets from he others what he himself needs. A family is *the* fundamental social group.

There are other groups that do not qualify as family. We call them households, or social clubs or fraternities/sororities, etc. Many of them are healthy and provide for the specific needs of their members. But they are not called "families" because their *raison d'etre* is different and more limited.

A family is special. It is hard to duplicate, and nature/nurture notwithstanding, it certainly contributes to serenity, or detracts from it.

I'm reminded of a widow I met in a bereavement group a few years ago. She was young, with three small children. She and her husband had moved here from the Midwest. His death overwhelmed her. It's trite to say she lost her serenity.

Even though her husband was no longer a living and present member, hers could still be called a family, maybe not the traditional family, but still a family. Yet something was missing for her, and she decided to move "to be with her family." She needed the community and haven that her family of origin could provide.

A family is special. When the four needs are not met, even though the essential roles are physically present, then everyone suffers. That's what happens to an alcoholic family. The characters that make the traditional family are there, but not the *characteristics* of parenting, training, community and haven.

Modern America is made up of many variations of "family." The list grows: the traditional families, stepfamilies, gay-parent families, single parent families, unmarried adults living together with or without children, grandparents caring for grandchildren, his-hers-and our children with three sets of parents, foster families, adoptive families, etc.

We need a clear definition of what "family" means. The words "good "and "bad" no longer tell us anything. In place of *judging* whether the family is good or not, we should understand that no matter who the cast of characters is that live together, it is rather the *characteristics* of that group that count. To describe a family, we may need to use a whole bunch of words instead of the two old stand-bys—good and bad.

Vincent B. Cardarelli, Th.M., CADC

    A family is a *family* when it provides for the parenting needs of dependent children when they are present. It is a family when it provides training and education, both physical, emotional and spiritual for adults as well as for children. It is a family when by its customs and rituals, it provides a sense of belonging and "communion" to one another. And a family is a *family* when each will love and accept one another, thereby providing protection and haven for those who "labor and are burdened."

8. CHILDREN AND SERENITY

In The Right Environment,
Children can have serenity too.

During a recent holiday, I had the good fortune to spend some time with families with growing children, ages varied between 6 and 12.

The thought came to me, how about children and serenity? Can growing children be at peace and at home in their surroundings?

At least in the families that I visited, it seemed that it was so. The children strolled from dining room to family room, from parents to friends, from one activity to another without anxiety or scrambling to gain the attention they needed.

They seemed to have the same rights and privileges as the adults without resorting to disruptive behavior.

Around the same time, I happened upon an article entitled "The Most Elusive Love Of All," by Sue Monk Kidd. She writes about a project that her 10-year old daughter was working on, a booklet on Four Ways to Love a Child. Her daughter had listed four rules for parents, each one accompanied by a crayon drawing.

The first one: "Go see chipmunks and stuff like that with your kids." Ms. Kidd realized that she "had been

Vincent B. Cardarelli, Th.M., CADC

treating the kids more like interruptions than family members whose lives I wanted to share and enjoy."

Sure, it is *our* job as parents to show our children ways that they should love us. But here was a child telling her mother how to love *her.* The meaning is to take the time, or better yet take time out, to pay attention to the child and what the child considers to be important.

The second rule said: "When kids mess up, give them some hugs." Another crayon drawing showing mom and child hugging. What do we usually do? Banish them to their room, get angry, lecture? Imagine the assurance that's given with a hug instead.

Number three, with an appropriate drawing, was: "Give kids a chance to talk."

Ms. Kidd thought about all the lectures she had given, and she out-talks the kids without giving them a chance to get a word in edgewise. If we want our children to "let us in," then we have to give them a chance to talk and we have to listen.

"Laugh a lot," was number four. Laughter puts a lot things into perspective, like sibling rivalry, water fights, and unintentional accidents like spilled milk.

Then Sue Monk Kidd writes a memorable paragraph which I copy in full below.

> "I closed the booklet. Yes, the children had been difficult. But so had I—hoarding time without sharing it, disciplining without loving, lecturing without listening, even forgetting my sense of humor. In that moment, I knew that the love I showed in the small, nitty-gritty moments of whines and water fights, grumbles and interruptions, may be the most elusive of all—and the most important."

How wise of both daughter and mother! These rules create an atmosphere—a climate—which invites serenity.

But—these rules for parents do not 'come naturally."

Parents need to take time out, pay attention, put things into perspective. As parents, we need to be less concerned about the rules that the children must follow, and heed the "rules" that we ourselves should follow.

Serenity can be for children, too. When they feel accepted, are listened to (which is not the same as getting their way) and feel like they are equal partners in a family, then the children are being nurtured in a climate that fosters serenity. They are allowed to feel a peaceful and restful spirit rather than one that is anxious and restless.

The "elusive kind of love" is a guarantor for serenity in children.

9. TWO DIARY ENTRIES ABOUT MY STEPFAMILY

Although fictitious, the following creation is 'based on fact."

Diary Entry: January 1994

I want to tell you, dear diary, about my family and my dilemma. I need to sort out my situation. I now live in a Stepfamily. Yes, that's right, a stepfamily. I just learned that "step" comes from the Old English word, "stoep" which means "orphaned."

I was so depressed for a long time when my parents separated and divorced four years ago. I can still remember it and I still harbor hopes that Mom and Dad will get back together again, although not as strongly as I used to.

Anyway, I live with my sister Karen, who is 10 (I'm 15), my mom, Carol, and my stepfather, Phil. They have been married for 2 years now. It's getting better, but in the beginning there was a lot of anger and hostility. You know, walking around the house with a mad face and not talking to one another. It felt like a cold war—and to tell you the truth, I don't even know why.

We live in Hunterdon County in a home that my mother and real father, Jim, bought when they were first married. There are lots of memories in this house. Every once in a while I sneak into the hall closet where the pictures of our family are stored. I can't believe that all those smiles and times of happiness have come to an end. I remember Dad coming in every night and kissing me on the forehead, after he thought I was asleep.

Dad is remarried to Kathy and they have a three month old baby boy. They've been married over a year. Since then Karen and I have not seen Dad as much, and we both miss him. We used to visit regularly every other week-end, when we did all kinds of fun things like go into the city; but I guess that's all in the past now.

My stepfather, Phil, was married before also. He had three children with his first wife. She is also remarried and lives in the mid-west with her husband and Phil's kids. The three kids come to visit in the summer for a couple of weeks. Wow! Is that a scene! The oldest boy, Jeff, hasn't come in the past few years, because he is planning to be married. One of the problems that we have been talking about in the family is whether or not we will go to the wedding. I can't really tell anybody, but I just do NOT want to go.

I HATE those kids, let me tell you. Phil tends to pussy-foot around them when they are here and yet he is strict with Karen and me. I guess he is afraid that his own kids will not like him anymore, if he lays down the law with them. He looks like he wants to pay back for what he put them through when he divorced their mother. Once I tried to talk to Mom about these feelings, but she seemed to take it upon herself to protect Phil and so I have just avoided the subject.

During Christmas, Mom tried to follow some of the customs that we used to do as a family when I was small. But Phil seemed to resent it and it caused an argument. I guess he felt that were imitating our previous family life.

Also during the holidays, Karen and I went to see Dad for an overnight. I got real mad when he and Kathy went out at night and used us as baby sitters. I also resent Kathy telling me what to do. She is not my mom and I want to be loyal to my own mother. I don't want to hurt my Dad, but since they have different rules from my own home, sometimes it seems that I am disrespectful. Then, I see Dad and Kathy sitting close to one another, giggling like young lovers, and I even feel jealous to some extent. (That sound childish, as I write it, but it is the truth.) I even feel like competing with her, like two cheerleaders fighting over a football hero.

But in spite of all this, dear Diary, I really want to make this into a family. I have strong feelings that pop up, and I don't know what to do with them. I usually go someplace by myself, or I write to you. It helps me to write, and maybe I'll adjust to this situation. I hope so, because that's what I really want.

Diary Entry: January 2001.

Well, dear Diary, looking back over these 6 years, I can't believe that I have come so far. Phil and Mom are together, and doing very well. I can even see why she divorced Dad, and it doesn't feel bad now. In fact, we get along quite well now. The "extended family" includes a lot of people, and when holidays come around we are surely a busy group.

We have evolved some new rituals, for birthdays, and anniversaries, and to some extent it is less expensive. You see, since there are so many, we have had to be creative in observing the important dates.

Dad's wife, Kathy, and I are comfortable with one another, even though we will never be close like I am with Mom.

The next event is my forthcoming marriage. It will be interesting to see how everyone handles that!

But at least we are all much more comfortable with one another than 6 years ago—talk about Serenity.

Section IV—Therapy and Mental Health

1. COUNSELING IS SOMETIMES USED TO REGAIN SERENITY

A significant number of people seek therapy when some conflict or trauma has visited them. For many, therapy helps them to regain peace in their lives, and provides them with strategies to cope with their problems.

So it makes sense to ask: What is therapy? I will explain my own answer to that question, but hasten to advise you that other therapists will have different answers.

First, I believe that therapy is the majority of cases should be short-term.

Yes, some patients need long-term therapy, because of the nature of their illnesses, or because of the serious wounds of childhood. I have indeed worked for long periods of time with such patients.

But for the greater number of "walking wounded," therapy (for me) means deciding on a reachable goal within a predictable amount of time, and then working together on a plan to reach that goal.

The temptation and the danger of long-term therapy is that a dependency develops between therapist and patient which can be counter-productive.

Therapy is successful only when the patient is "free"— free from the shackles of his illness, free from addictions,

Vincent B. Cardarelli, Th.M., CADC

free from self-destructive patterns, and free from his need to depend upon the therapist.

He is, in short, free to stand on his own two feet.

Continual "checking it out" with a therapist or a group is a characteristic of adolescence, when one looks to an authority to help solve problems.

I also believe that there are two stages to therapy:

The first stage is symbolized by the word "why."

In the beginning of counseling, insight is necessary. It is important to ask the whys and wherefores and to look into the past. If we don't pay attention to history, we are bound to repeat it.

But it is easy to become obsessed by "why"—since every "why" has a "because," and every "because" has another "why."

And on and on it goes.

The "why" stage must lead to the second and more important stage in therapy which is symbolized by the word "what."

What do I feel? What is happening? And what am I going to do about it? Another way of saying that is, we need to "walk the walk, and not just talk the talk."

Some change in behavior or some action must be taken to rise above the defense mechanisms, the inadequate style of the past, or the personality defects that keep one from being free to grow.

No one is perfect, that's true; but there are many problems that we can overcome, and it is only when we move from "why" to "what" that we release the energy to make a change.

Therapy is popular today, with many referrals being made. I think the reason for that is due in part to fact that people do not use religion for guidance and support as they once did.

The purpose of religion is to show us the way and to free us from bondage when we get bogged down. Religion makes us feel like we are "children of God, children of the universe, with a sense of belonging and a purpose to life."

Often that is exactly what I provide in counseling—a support and a boost to one's self-esteem, a sense that one can overcome the chains binding us to childhood, or to a bad marriage or to a job which makes life miserable.

In the past, our need for self-esteem and acceptance was fulfilled by churches and synagogues. They did so by rituals, by traditions and by men who taught in the name of God. Belonging to a faith group helped them cope with life, and made sense out of it.

Today, many seek this kind of help in therapy.

A final thought: As therapy progresses, a relationship develops between therapist and patient. The relationship should be "therapeutic," i.e. a model of how healthy people interact with one another.

Therapy is not only an intellectual exercise, but it also provides a "corrective emotional experience (Franz Alexander)."

The patient has an experience in the session which he can apply to the important people and issues in his life.

Thus, confrontation with the therapist, or learning how to compromise, or to restate some misunderstanding are all part of the process of therapy, so that the patient can transfer that interaction into his 'real" life.

If we wish to grow into adults, we must take responsibility for our actions. Despite an unhappy childhood. Despite dysfunctional families. Despite sexual and physical abuse. Despite life's cruel and random traumas.

We are responsible, and accepting responsibility is a sure-fire way of attaining serenity.

2. DISEASE OR BAD HABIT

Labeling emotional problems is "good news...bad news"

    Mental and emotional disorders interfere with one's serenity and happiness. These disorders have been identified and given medical names, called diagnoses. There are 374 (at last count) in the DSM (Diagnostic and Statistical Manual.)

    But "brand new diseases," says John Leo (U.S. News and World Report), "including a lot of implausible ones" are being added to the DSM that already lists almost 400 official disorders that psychiatrists and insurance companies recognize.

    For example, says Mr. Leo, "News reports say that 'road rage' is on the brink of being certified as an official mental disorder...Until now most of us have assumed that drivers who cut us off and give us the finger are just irate swine. But no, they appear to be suffering from a mental disorder, just like schizophrenics."

    The same author goes on to list other candidates: caffeine-induced anxiety disorder, telephone scatologia (sexual phone calls), thinking about a former lover, holding a grudge and feeling apprehensive about giving a speech. "The DSM is converting nearly all life's stresses and bad habits into mental disorders."

There is also the "new talk about 'shadow syndromes,' or mild versions of serious ailments." That is, they do not yet qualify as disorders according to the DSM, but need to be included in it. "New disorders do for psychiatrists what the litigation boom did for lawyers."

I don't fully agree with Mr. Leo. There are advantages to putting a label on a mental disorder. First of all, the insurance companies will pay for treatment. One who is suffering from mental or emotional disease is just as entitled to treatment as one who suffers from diabetes or high blood pressure. Another advantage is that the patient who presents with an identifiable disease feels exonerated, and the stigma is removed. He/she is not just "crazy."

When a client comes to me, and I can label it "alcoholism" (or whatever), then that helps him to accept what has befallen him without blame, and we can get on to the work of therapy, i.e. overcoming the illness. He didn't "do it to himself."

However, there are also disadvantages to the labeling process. First, while labeling takes away blame, it may also give the person an excuse to prolong the suffering. "It's not my fault." The patient still has to accept responsibility for getting better; the label is not an excuse.

Further, says Mr. Leo, and with this I do agree, "the effort and the concepts behind (the labeling) are seeping deep into the culture, reinforcing the *victim* industry and teaching us to look for psychiatric answers to every social and personal problem. It's easier to sedate an alleged Attention Deficit Hyperactive Disorder youngster with Ritalin than to do something about the environment—family and/or school—that might explain his behavior."

Finally, if life experiences that are essential for learning humility, maturity and serenity are labeled "diseases," then we miss the opportunity of learning how to cope with the human condition. On the contrary, we are learning—in fact, encouraged - to eradicate it, medicate it or blame someone else for its existence and solution.

Vincent B. Cardarelli, Th.M., CADC

It's true: we want mental and emotional disorders to receive the same kind of treatment and insurance coverage as other illnesses. But to call life stressors and bad habits "disorders or diseases" postpones or even prevents "growing up." As long as we can blame a disease for our woes, it is very likely that we will look for the solution "outside of us—in prescriptions, or drugs, or alcohol, or in another person.

Counselors need to accept the responsibility of teaching clients to become responsible for their own lives.

3. ORIGINAL SCRIPT

To What Extent Is My Life An Original Script?

Some years ago I saw a movie called *Affliction* with Nick Nolte and James Coburn. It told a disturbing story about the legacy that an abusive father leaves behind for his son. The script of the father seems destined to be repeated in the son.

The film reminded me of something that I once read which went like this: There are only three of four scripts according to which everyone lives his life. But each person lives his own script as if it were an *original.*

In other words, many lives are predictably similar, yet each of us believes that "my" life is special and different from all others. Many say: "I'll never be like my parents." And yet, after years pass, and one looks back, there are many similarities.

But there are also significant differences.

As a result, each person has to learn for himself, and parents soon realize, often with disappointment, that they cannot effectively prevent their children from making the same mistakes they made. Hermann Hesse's novel *Siddhartha* tells the story of a father who learned this lesson the hard way.

Vincent B. Cardarelli, Th.M., CADC

I look at my life and I see similarities to my father's. The values we lived by, the habits acquired, the choices we made (e.g. marriage late in life.) And yet I don't feel that I am reliving his life—my own is uniquely my own.

I heat stories of countless clients, many of which are replays of others before them. Yet it would be heartless of me to compare one to the other, or to predict the outcome based on another "script." It simply would not work for me as a counselor to tell a client "Look, you're just like so-and-so, and you should do x-y-z because that is what worked for her and it will work for you."

History and experience show us that lives do evolve in similar patterns; in a sense, there is nothing new under the sun. Yet despite that, there are enough individual and idiosyncratic incidents in each one's life to make it an original. Even though there is a predictability to life, each person's experience is as different from others as snowflakes are from one another.

"A life is sacred only to the person who happens to be living it," says author Gerry Blake. It's true, you know. What happens to you is very important, no matter what it may mean to someone else.

Even though your life may be the same as so many others, and even though what you do and decide is predictable and commonplace, yet your life is unique and it is YOU who look out at the world and experience it as your own in a special way. As the poem *Desiderata* says, "you are a child of the universe, and you belong here."

It's true of twins, although they may be separated, very similar things happen to them at exactly the same time; and yet they are different. And it will be true of clones, if ever that comes to pass, no matter how alike they may be.

It is a strange balancing act that I—and you—have to perform: on the one hand, I am one of a bunch—all you have to do is walk the streets of New York, shoulder to shoulder with masses of people, to realize how many there are of "us" that belong to that bunch—and on the other hand, even though I am indistinguishable in that crowd, I just know that I am *different*. I am ME!

In order to maintain that balancing act, you need to avoid two extremes. On one side of the spectrum, you need to avoid an exaggerated sense of self, which makes you SO different that you would be narcissistic, and a God unto yourself. The other extreme to avoid is a low self-esteem which says that you are so common that there is nothing exceptional about you. Both extremes are unhealthy, and prevent serenity.

Your serenity depends on your ability to say and believe: "I'm O.K., you're O.K. I'm not perfect, and neither are you—but THAT's O.K." I'm not better than you, and you're not better than me. I won't take advantage of you, nor will I let you take advantage of me. You and I are different; but my difference is *uniquely* my own.

In a very real sense, your script, your life, is a blend of what is common to so many others, and of what is special to you. To that extent, your life is an original.

4. I MADE A MISTAKE? — or — I AM A MISTAKE?

"I can live with guilt but not with shame. Guilt is funny, shame is tragic. Guilt nags, shame stabs."

"Guilt is when I haven't called my mother; shame is when I'm not a good mother."

"It's easier to tell you what I am guilty about, but my shame is my secret."

"Guilt motivates, shame paralyzes." (These quotes are from *Family Circle* magazine.)

The modern day oracle, John Bradshaw, writes: "Guilt says, 'I made a mistake,' while shame says, 'I am a mistake.'"

Guilt is a reactive feeling to something I did that was wrong; Shame is a wound in the soul that no amount of forgiveness will alleviate.

Guilt is like putting on new jeans and then getting splattered with mud. You can wash it off and feel clean again. Shame is like putting on new jeans and even though they are spotless, you still feel stained and dirty. No amount of "washing" will heal that wound.

Guilt is a natural way station in the development of a child toward maturity and adulthood. Everyone feels guilt, for example, at breaking rules, at making a mistake, at goofing up. In a sense, guilt goes with the territory. Eventually, as one grows, guilt as a motivator gives way to more noble emotions, like caring and commitment.

Shame, however, is toxic; it is a violation of the process of growing up. Sometimes, people use the word shame, as in "I am ashamed," when they mean embarrassed. In that sense, it is a valuable emotion.

But the toxic shame that I wish to spotlight now is a subtle form of abuse of power by parents, or by representatives of the church, or by those who speak with some authority, like teachers and even by social workers.

Just think of the effects on children by the commonplace and inconsiderate remarks we level at them: "What's the matter with you, dummy?" "You'll never amount to anything, lazyhead!" "God! What a mistake you turned out to be!" "I'll never be able to trust you again!" "Hey, stupid!"

Should I go on? The effect of these put-downs is just as serious—maybe even more so- than sexual and physical abuse, precisely because they are subtle and not so obvious. Except when you stop to think about them.

When we can point to a clear and definite abuse of a child, at least we can identify the 'perpetrator' and help the child absolve the feeling of blaming himself. But when the perpetrator is invisible, the effect of "shaming" strikes at the internal vulnerable self.

Another example is when the child is brought for therapy. The "helping" person is expected to look for a diagnosis: i.e. to look for what is wrong with the child that is the cause of his problem. (Incidentally, there is no medical diagnosis for "shame.")

Now, obviously, it is an exaggeration to say that in every case the child is suffering from toxic shame. But it is not an exaggeration to say that often enough, when a child has suffered from shame, then he will act as if he "is a mistake."

The "wounded child" is crying out for a healing ministration, not a continuing message that there is "something wrong with him."

Vincent B. Cardarelli, Th.M., CADC

Therapy for shame needs to involve not only the child, but also the parents and maybe even the school. The equally sad part is that when children are given the message of shame, they carry it through life, and it often shows up in their marriage, or in the way they discipline their own children later on.

The legacy of guilt can be erased by making amends, but the legacy of shame is more intractable. Guilt make us co-dependents; but shame makes us perennially unhappy. It is important to know the difference between guilt and shame.

5. COMPLEX PROBLEMS
Modern Day Problems Have Become More Complicated

When I first started working as a therapist in 1972, the problems my patients presented seemed much less complicated than today.

The average number of outpatient visits to our clinic at the time was five. Some came more often, but many came fewer than five times. The more serious problems were handled on an inpatient basis.

Most were handled on a one hour a week basis. The most frequent problems presented were uncomplicated alcoholism, depression, conduct disorders and school phobias (for children).

Today, however, these problems still exist, but in a more severe way. Alcoholism is not just alcoholism. Alcohol abusers are usually addicted to more than one substance; and further they may be dually diagnosed, i.e. have two severe disorders coexisting.

An adolescent is not just unhappy or maladjusted or acting out in school; he doesn't just get caught running down the hall, or chewing gum in the classroom. It is more complex—he is thinking about suicide or coping with unhappiness by experimenting with alcohol or drugs. He may be overwhelmed by feelings of anger or frustration, with no way to express those feelings adequately. A teen may have formed an intimate relationship before he was emotionally capable of handling it; and a break-up will cause trauma. Many are drinking and driving, putting themselves and others at risk.

Depression is no longer just depression. It is complicated with various forms of anxiety, and often this condition is incorrectly diagnosed and medicated. It used to be that a widow was just expected to wear black for awhile and ask for help from her extended family who lived nearby and were free to help out since they were not working.

Not so today. Now it is "post-traumatic stress disorder" with serious economic, job-related and social ramifications. Add to that the fact that family members live far-away, or are themselves working or off to college and are unavailable.

Memory recalls that a young man who got into trouble could "plea bargain" himself into two or three years of military service, and then come out of that experience a grown-up man, ready for a job and marriage. The structure provided by the service was enough to allow him time to mature.

Not so today. Not only does the military not take him, but should he need some structure to help him solve his problems, he would have to go off to "Outward Bound" or a rehab center or a residential school. Of course, this is complicated and very expensive.

Further, some researchers maintain that in today's society, a young person does not mature until he is into his twenties, given the complexity of what he has to experience and learn for success in life.

Think about the prevalence of AIDS, or other sexually transmitted diseases, of the ubiquity of impulse control disorders, such as Attention Deficit Hyperactive Disorder (ADHD), and addictions, like anorexia, drugs and smoking. Think about the increase in the numbers of poor who do not have insurance. Listen to talk shows as they showcase the ravages of divorce on the marriage partners as well as the children.

Once you add all this up and begin to imagine the complex nature of the problems that people present to the therapist, psychiatrist or family doctor, you can begin to get a picture of the multi-faceted and intricate crises that are handled in the office.

To be sure, the techniques and medications that have been introduced into treatment have also become more complex and effective. But more serious problems take more time to treat.

One of the points that I'd like to make is that, together with the growth of more complex problems, there has arisen a "quick fix" mentality. The expectation is that there is not only an answer to every problem, but a sure-fire quick one. There is a general impatience in the air, an impulsivity to get it done.

"Therapy" has indeed become more acceptable since it doesn't have the stigma of the past. But the expectation—as it was in the past—is still the same, namely that a few sessions will be sufficient—and if not, well, then "it doesn't work."

The hope for a magical cure is ever-present. It is almost the same as when a child scrapes his knee and runs to his mother crying: "Please make it stop hurting."

In the past, a therapist more often than not could give almost immediate relief if not a solution—a Band-Aid approach. But today, with the complexity that life adds to what were formerly "normal" problems, therapy is not only more intricate, but it is also more lengthy.

Of course, not everyone turns to therapy for solutions. Most people are able to live their own lives without outside help. But when you do turn to therapy, it takes patience and courage to dedicate yourself to recovery—for the patient as well as for the therapist.

6. PERFECTIONISM, BY BEING SELF-DEFEATING, PREVENTS SERENITY

There's a fair number of people who suffer from the symptom of *Perfectionism*. It is not a disorder by itself, but a symptom shared by different personalities. And it is experienced in varying degrees: from the annoying to the truly incapacitating.

David D. Burns, M.D., says that perfectionists are those "whose standards are high beyond reach or reason, people who strain compulsively and unremittingly toward impossible goals and who measure their own worth <u>entirely in terms of productivity and accomplishment.</u> For these people, the drive to excel can only be self-defeating."

This article does not refer to the pursuit of excellence by men and women who find satisfaction in striving to do their best, and who stand out from the crowd as heroes or leaders in their field. There's nothing unhealthy about that, and in fact, discoveries and advances in life are due to such men. People like Einstein, Madam Curie, etc.

The perfectionist, however, is the person who goes to the extreme is never satisfied, and thus pays a high price for his compulsion: troubled relationships, low self-esteem, serious mood disorders, anxieties and decreased productivity. And so, instead of making a person produce more and feel better, perfectionism is actually self-defeating.

It's called the *saint or sinner syndrome.* If you don't perform perfectly, then you're no good; you're a failure. A perfectionist measures his own worth by his accomplishments. If you perform well, then you're OK. The trouble is that when he judges his own performance, he rarely comes up to his own expectations—in taking tests, in doing his work, in being a parent, or a writer, etc.

And paradoxically, the harder they try, the less they do, because they are not satisfied by the results. So they have to start again, postpone the effort, or put the work aside until they can do better. And so, perfectionists are hindered or even incapacitated (e.g. writer's block) by the very urge to do the best they can.

Perfectionists are plagued by some mental distortions (otherwise called "stinking thinking"). The first is **all or nothing thinking.** They evaluate everything in black or white, good or bad. Very little gray area exists. It's the saint or sinner complex. "If I don't come in first, (or if I'm not right in my opinion), then I'm no good." Something as insignificant as a slight criticism on a work evaluation can throw a perfectionist into a demoralized state. He needs to **win,** because losing is a personal failure.

A second distortion is **a fear of appearing foolish or inadequate.** And so making a mistake is a "failure"—something that has the weight of a kernel of pop-corn has the effect of a brick. "I can't afford to be wrong." Imagine what happens in a marriage if one of the partners always has to be right—better yet, if **both** have to be right.

A third distortion is **overgeneralization.** "I'm *always* goofing up." "The world *stinks.*" "I'm *never* going to get it right." In this case, the tail wags the dog; what ought to be insignificant becomes all-important.

A fourth distortion is what is called "the tyranny of the **should."** They are plagued by statements such as: "I should have...I should do better...I must never do that again." They are trapped in moralistic judgments, mostly about themselves, but sometimes about others as well. They go round and round in their heads about how they could have done better, or how they can avoid making the same mistake in the future. As a result, guilt is a constant companion.

A perfectionist's self-esteem is contingent upon approval or success. One criticism is enough to cause a crisis in how she feels about herself. (He or she).

What can you do about this unnecessary burden? Many will answer that you can go to counseling (or to confession.) Yes, that will certainly help. But before you do, try this four-part self-help program:

1. Become aware of both the price (disadvantages) as well as the benefits (advantages) of trying to be perfect. Make a list and balance out the costs and the benefits. For example: one client listed the benefits as "I'll produce fine work which I'll be proud of." But the costs were: "I'll be uptight...I'm afraid to take risks...I become self-critical of myself as well as of others." So for her, it became cost effective to lower her expectations.
2. Practice leaving something unfinished til the next day. And as you go on, practice leaving something 'imperfect'—in your moral life as well as your productive life.
3. Reprogram your 'all or nothing thinking'—your "stinking thinking." The world does not divide itself into two categories: all-good versus all-bad. There are many gray areas in between. Everyone—yes, **everyone** - falls in between. Imperfection is normal, perfection is impossible.
4. Finally, keep a record of your self-critical thoughts and statements. See how many times you use words like 'stupid', or 'wrong', or 'messed up' or 'mistake' etc. See how often you compare yourself to others and come up short.

Then aim for "average", "adequate" "good enough". Force yourself to be satisfied with less than perfect

You're not a second-rate person if you don't come in first. **You** are not a mistake if you make a mistake; you are human, not flawed.

A Retreat Master once told me: when you go to a dog track, the dogs race after a mechanical rabbit. They never catch the rabbit (reach the goal), but just think of all the ground they cover in *trying.*

7. MEN NEED A SECOND CHANCE

I do quite a bit of marriage counseling. A major part of counseling couples involves "training"—training in learning how to communicate effectively.

That is no easy task, because it involves making a change, both for men and women. To start off with, both are sincerely convinced they know how to communicate, even though their first words are: "We don't communicate too well."

The point of this article is that women seem to take to the process of therapy better than men. Women seem to 'catch on' quickly; whereas men find it unsettling, if not down-right irritating, to have to back-up and, in a sense, start over.

I am here asking women to give men a chance—a second chance, as it were.

Women not only seem to have the jump on communication, they indeed have a distinct advantage. There are reasons for that.

The first reason is that by nature and by tradition, a woman is a nurturing person. The man is the Provider, Protector and Progenitor. His role has traditionally been to see a problem and then to solve it; never mind talking about it. What good does that do?

TOWARD SERENITY

And so when a conflict arises between husband and wife, the man's natural tendency is to rise to the occasion and "solve" it. He does this by a knee-jerk reaction. His wife wants to "talk" about it. He doesn't see the point of it; she gets angry and blames him for not "listening.

When they enter counseling, it seems that when I show them their past habitual way of communicating, and present another way, the woman is able to "pick it up" more quickly.

Another reason why she finds it easier to try something different (and I got this idea from a friend of mine) is that she already had a "second chance" at working on a relationship from an emotional side. She gets pregnant and "feels" for nine months. That is an experience that a man never has.

Both man and woman had their first chance with their parents while growing up. But when she gets pregnant, and nurses the baby in the first few months, she gets another chance. The wife/mother has to learn to speak a word-less language for a period of time. This amounts to a built-in opportunity to communicate emotionally, and do it right if she didn't the "first time."

The father/husband stands by while this is happening. Not only that, but often enough the father/husband is "in the way" during the first few months, and sometimes for the first few years. The baby, in a sense, temporarily usurps his father's primary place in providing emotional satisfaction for its mother. The husband meanwhile misses that chance.

I remember some years ago a client coming to me and honestly but with embarrassment confessing that he was not only jealous of his baby son, but also he began to dislike him. He felt like an outsider. He felt that his son had taken his place.

Well, I ask you, with whom can a father share *that* thought and "be understood?"

He would be told, "You shouldn't feel like that!" And so he hides or denies his feelings. While he is trying to hide his feelings, his wife is happily describing her feelings (which she "should") to one and all.

Up to the time a couple comes for marriage counseling, the man has had only one chance to 'get it right,' and that was as a child with his mother. So when they come for counseling, it's like a "second chance." His wife may have had several chances.

Back when the roles between husband and wife were pretty clearly outlined and strictly observed, the husband was indeed the problem-solver. (OK, most of the time.) But in the last 30 or so years, the roles have become indistinct and, in many cases, interchangeable. So yes, in come cases men have had a second chance, due to the circumstances.

Often I see a couple where the wife is making twice the salary as her husband. Or a husband who is a stay-at-home parent; or as often happens today, a husband who shares parenting and housework. Men have done pretty well in catching up to the new roles expected of them, but it may take them somewhat longer to become proficient in learning a new language, a language that expresses emotions.

So sometimes, if the man acts like a *man*, that is, *macho*, he is considered abusive, either verbally or emotionally. Rightly so, we "should not" accept that. But if a woman acts "emotionally", that is what she "should" do, and we do accept that. In this sense, then, a man may need a second chance.

This is not meant to be an *apologia* on behalf of men; it is meant to help both men and women to *understand* why a man needs a second chance, too.

Women need understanding, absolutely; but so do men. So in the therapy hour, women catch on more quickly than men; but that doesn't make them any better. It just makes them reach the finish line more quickly. Most of the men I have seen in counseling really do have a desire to learn how to communicate. If their wives are willing to wait around until he "catches on," there is much hope for a marriage that initially was fraught with conflict.

My limited experience has been that any couple who is willing to expend the energy to learn new ways of talking to one another, can step up to a new level of peace and harmony in their marriage.

Each of you deserves a second chance at strengthening your relationship.

8. MEN NEED A POSITIVE SELF—IMAGE TO EXPERIENCE SERENITY

I've been thinking about writing on the topic of men and serenity for some time. Along comes a book entitled STIFFED, and believe it or not, written by a noted feminist, which is subtitled THE BETRAYAL OF THE AMERICAN MALE.

Susan Faludi, the author, shows that the way men are evaluated has changed in the past fifty years, and she concludes that men have been "stiffed"—i.e., they have been betrayed by American society—not by their own fault, and not by the feminist movement, but by a society and culture that has developed since WWII.

Without realizing it, our society has changed the meaning of "masculinity" and as a result, men are confused about their role. A crisis has developed in men's self-image.

Events like the Promise Keepers conferences, and the Million Men March, show that men are trying to retrieve the "old" meaning of masculinity. Movements like these and others like Robert Bly's *Iron Man*, show that men are seeking to find a relevant image for themselves. But society does not allow men to be "masculine" in the old way.

At the end of World War II, men came back as heroes. They knew what they had to do to maintain respect both from themselves and from women. They went into industry, into technology, into large corporations. And these benevolent corporations promised them security, benefits, and jobs until they were ready to retire.

Men were clear about what they had to **do**, and since that was so, they were clear about who they **were**. **Being** and **doing** were the same. They could look themselves in the mirror and be proud. And women would be proud of their "men" as well.

But then came the 80's and 90's with downsizing, and moving families all over the place, and men became expendable. No longer were they secure that if they "did their job" and "provided for their family" ands "kept a stiff upper lip" in the face of adversity; and even if they went to war, as in Vietnam, they were not allowed to be proud of that. **Being** and **doing** were no longer the same; it was no longer so clear what a man had to **do** in order to **be** a man.

It didn't make any difference if men were brave and faithful, it could all go up in smoke in the stroke of a pen. Between 1995 and 1997, 8 million men were laid off as a result of changes in society in ways of doing business and in making a profit.

As a result, a generalized resentment built up among American men. Who were men supposed to blame? What was happening wasn't even noticed. At least when women in the past couple of centuries began their fight for equality and respect in the marketplace, they had **men** to blame. So it's almost natural that men now blame women for their plight—not just women, but **feminists.**

Faludi says: "The day Ernie Pyle died could well have been the day Ernie Pyle's stoical man died and the Century of the Common Man was stillborn. No one knew it yet...American society changed from one that produced a culture to a culture rooted in no real society at all."

In other words, American culture had "defined manhood by character, by the inner qualities of stoicism, integrity, reliability, the ability to shoulder burdens, the willingness to put others first, the desire to protect and provide and sacrifice." If you think about it, these "nurturing" qualities are amazingly similar to what we attribute to *motherhood*.

But that society changed and so did the culture that it spawned. The "culture rooted in no real society" became an "ornamental culture," in which manhood "is defined by appearance, by youth and attractiveness, by money and aggression, by posture and swagger and "props," by the curled lip and petulant sulk and flexed biceps, by the glamour of the cover boy, and by the market-bartered "individuality" that sets one astronaut or athlete or gangster above a another."

In an ornamental culture, men do not experience brotherhood, which is probably what the Promise Keepers are seeking. There is no loyalty or satisfaction in working together toward a common goal, the lack of which is so evident in professional sports—the era of the super-star. There is no over-arching goal such as patriotism or love of country; or helping to make successful the corporation for which men work.

God forbid that man should give up a lucrative job offer if it interfered with his family; or refuse to relocate. Or just be satisfied with **being** a Common Man.

The "masculine promise" of 1945 dissipated into the shell of empty promises and unfulfilled expectations. Women are not the culprit, nor is it affirmative action. And men are not themselves to blame; they didn't even realize what was happening. According to Faludi, what has happened is a social and cultural tragedy, and a betrayal of the American male.

And so, dear reader, (if you have stayed with this chapter to this point) men's image of themselves has suffered a collective blow.

We men have to take the reins and fashion a new definition of masculinity for Y2K, one which will give us as much pride in ourselves as the pride that GI's had going off to war, and coming back victorious; as the pride of post-war workers who labored with the goal of a home and family and a job that would last until they retired.

A new definition of masculinity which allows men to have a positive image, instead of an ornamental one, will contribute to their serenity.

Faludi calls for a national discussion which hopefully will fashion a culture that affirms the needs of both men and women alike.

9. RESILIENCY: AN ESSENTIAL ELEMENT OF SERENITY

The dictionary defines Resiliency as: the ability to recover quickly from illness, change or misfortune; buoyancy. I call it *bounce-back-ability.*

When confronted with some trauma, or stressor, it's very common for people to be overwhelmed, or temporarily thrown off balance. For some, the event may be seriously debilitating, and knock them out of commission. So knowing that one will bounce back, and knowing *how* to bounce back—**resiliency**—is like having an insurance policy to regain serenity.

Some people are by nature resilient; but some need training to learn how to bounce back, and not stay mired in trouble.

Training in resiliency requires first that you get into the habit of asking the right questions: "what?" questions instead of "why?" questions. What is really going on with me? With my children? Instead of: Why did this happen to me? Why did he do this? "Why?" looks backward; "What?" looks forward. "Why?" looks for reasons; "What?" looks for solutions. What can I do about it?

Another habit to get into is to *get started*, a "do it, dammit" attitude. Remember *Dead Poets' Society?* The password was **Carpe diem**, which in Latin means "seize the day," or "make hay while the sun shines." In other words, don't just sit there and think about it (why did this happen?), do something. Getting started is half the job, the other half is to stick with it.

Resiliency training teaches people to take the initiative, to take charge of problems. You are to guard against a passive attitude, one of just accepting what happens and waiting for God or whomever to help you out of the mess. In general, it means to have an optimistic perspective when looking at the stressful events; a feeling that you can do something about it and have some influence on the outcome.

Resilient people are challenged by new experiences rather than frightened by them. And even if they are anxious and frightened, they overcome the threat they feel and "get going." They screw up their courage and face the fear of the unknown, rather than let the circumstances dictate what happens next. Resilient people bounce back after a setback, and don't feel sorry for themselves.

The ability to look on life as a challenge is particularly difficult to acquire since it needs a personality change. But it can be done! Maybe not with a batting average of 100%, but enough to make life more enjoyable.

Finally, a sense of humor helps when nothing else works. A sense of humor is different from being a comedian. A comedian makes people laugh; to have a sense of humor is to be able to laugh at oneself, and not take oneself so seriously.

I think it is true to say that life is more challenging today, jobs more stressful, family life more worrisome. As a result, people have to become more resilient, more self-reliant, more flexible than even before.

Trying to tap into one's innate resources of resiliency is like a spiritual exercise. It reminds me of what I used to hear at retreats on spirituality. To train oneself in resiliency needs the same dedication that a long-distance runner needs to get into shape for track events.

Vincent B. Cardarelli, Th.M., CADC

In the book: **The Hardy Executive**, by Maddi and Kobasa, there's a chapter on counseling for resiliency. It is a hopeful section, since it says that people are not damned by an unfortunate childhood, or by tragedies. It's not easy to train oneself (either alone or with the help of an expert) in resiliency, but the hard work is rewarding.

10. PANIC ATTACKS: A TEAR IN THE FABRIC OF SERENITY

Panic attacks are a severe form of anxiety, and they seem to be very prevalent now. Panic prevents any semblance of serenity.

Many men and women, adults as well as adolescents, seem to be vulnerable to this scary type of anxiety, which can accurately be called "Panic," or "Panic Disorder."

A young man in his middle 20's is swimming in a pool Without warning, he experiences a frightening attack.

He is hit with pain like a heart attack, cannot breathe, feels his skin crawling.

After a check-up with his doctor, he is pronounced physically healthy. His symptoms, however, continue intermittently. He lives in terror of having the attacks return.

A young single mother tells her doctor that she is afraid she is going crazy. She has periodic attacks of panic, as if someone jumped out of the closet with a weapon. The last one happened in the line at the A&P. She can't figure out why they happen.

She is now beginning to avoid the several places where the attacks have occurred and lives in anticipation of the next one. Her life is controlled by fear, an irrational fear.

Vincent B. Cardarelli, Th.M., CADC

Most victims of panic attacks keep it a secret for a long time before they reach out for help. They are afraid that people will think they are crazy.

The symptoms of this disorder range from moderate ones, such as increased heartbeats and sweating, to severe ones, such as chest pain, hyperventilation and a dread of dying or going crazy. Other symptoms are a sense of unreality, choking sensations, pounding heart, blurred vision, hot and cold flashes, and a general fear of losing control.

Everyone wants to know "why?" these attacks occur. The causes, however, are not clear. There are a number of theories which seek to explain them.

One theory attributes the "conditioning" to associations with certain circumstances such as a crowded room, an automobile ride, or a certain fear from childhood (although unconscious.)

Psychoanalysis (a Freudian approach) attributes the origin of panic attacks to unresolved separation anxiety, i.e. threats of separation from parents, or disapproval of parents or authority figures.

And then there is the theory that says that there is NO cause; it is a false alarm stemming from the "fight-or-flight" instinct. It's like an electrical surge that upsets the balance.

Well, whatever you want to accept as reasonable, there is no doubt about the agony and suffering the victims experience.

Panic attacks do not follow a precise pattern in every person; some have occasional attacks and never develop the more severe disorder of agoraphobia. Some have lingering anxiety, but manage it with a stiff upper lip. But all suffer from anticipating the next attack; they live in knuckle-biting fear.

Despite the severity of the symptoms, there is definitely GOOD news: the treatment for panic disorder is eminently effective.

TOWARD SERENITY

Anti-depressant drugs work best in preventing the attacks from recurring. Anti-anxiety drugs may be used together with anti-depressants. There are a number of drugs available, and if one does not work, usually another will. They take two or three weeks to become effective.

Research has shown that drugs together with counseling produce the best results. "Talking" therapy by itself is not considered as effective. Supportive psychotherapy, together with drug therapy, includes behavioral and/or cognitive techniques. Usually a therapist conducts these sessions, although results can be achieved by tapes and groups. Variations of psychotherapy can include education or reading and relaxation techniques.

Desensitization is another type of therapy in which a therapist allows gradual exposure, under watchful guidance, to the situation that provokes the fear. As the program of exposure unfolds, the patient becomes more confident that the panic will not reoccur and begins to control his disorder.

Since there is now effective therapy to treat this debilitating illness, victims are strongly encouraged to seek help.

One of the reasons patients avoid going to the doctor is a sense of shame and embarrassment that accompanies these symptoms. That is unfortunate, since the illness is well known to family doctors. Confide in your doctor. He or she will understand. If necessary, you will be referred to a therapist who is knowledgeable, and in a relatively short time you will begin to have relief.

Both the young man and the single mom mentioned above are now symptom free.

Section V—Aging and Losses

1. LOSSES AND GRIEF

We experience losses all through our life. The first loss is that of the pristine surroundings of the womb. And from then on, whether we want them or not, losses are a part of life. The most traumatic loss is that of Death.

With every loss comes the "natural" reaction of *grief.* Grief is the emotion that loss produces: and although it is a difficult emotion, it is normal, and in a sense, necessary to experience it. Some will cope with death cautiously pretending it will not happen to them.

I have a theory: each one rehearses and practices a "style" of handling losses, which style is repeated at the time of death in an exaggerated manner. In other words, whenever you lose something, you tend to grieve in the same way and you will repeat that style of grief at the time of a relative's death—and eventually at your own death.

Examples: The way one copes with the loss of a friend who moves away is indicative of how he will cope with other major losses. The way one copes with the loss of youth when he ages, may well give some insight as to how he will cope with death.

Losses accompany us throughout life, beginning at birth. Then we are weaned from the bottle, another loss. You can make your own list of the losses you have experienced up to this point in your life: leaving home to go

Vincent B. Cardarelli, Th.M., CADC

to school; breaking away from parents; passing from the innocence of childhood into adolescence; getting married and losing independence; divorce; and so on into later stages where we lose friends, spouse and then life itself.

My point is simple: each of us has a certain way of handling these losses. If the loss is severe, the way we handle it will be the same but exaggerated in intensity.

Whatever the style may be, everyone usually experiences the same feelings, possibly in different degrees and for varying lengths of time. Grief is the emotional response that a person has to the loss and then to the realization that what was there is no longer there. You have to accustom yourself to detach from it, to learn to live without it, and then to reattach yourself to something in its place. You need to do that in order to continue to live and function in society.

The process is: *attach, detach, reattach, restore.* Someone (or something) who was important to you (attach) dies, you then need to let him (it) go (detach). Next you need to go on without that person by involving yourself in the new kind of world (reattach), and then live a life without the presence of the lost one (restore).

Basically, that whole process is called *grief.* It is a natural emotion, even though for many it will be the worst of all experiences. We would rather not experience grief, and sometimes use any means to avoid it, or postpone it. Grief is lonely, uncertain, fearful, morose, immobile, indecisive, panicky. It feels like one is constantly searching for the lost and loved one, with the urge to talk about him/her continually.

Some feel numb and disbelieving: "it can't possibly have happened." It produces anger and guilt; people lose appetite, weight and sleep. Some experience physical symptoms like heart palpitations, headaches and pain. There is a lump in one's stomach.

And yet—it is a "normal" reaction in the sense that it will not be denied. Grief needs a forum in which it can be felt and expressed. It is O.K. to "muck around" for awhile in sorrow and self-pity. A grieving person needs a supportive family, a friend, or group, who understand the complex emotions and don't have expectations that the person ought to get himself together and move forward with life. Maybe it needs a professional who calls the experience "life" rather than an illness such as depression.

In short, grief must be expressed. In time, it will be lessened.

I loved, which was Heaven.
I lost, which was Hell.
I survived, which is Life.

2. HANDLING LOSSES #1

How You Handle Your Losses Is a Key to Serenity

Some years ago I took a cruise on the Mississippi River on a grand steamboat, *The American Queen,* paddlewheel and all. It was a walk back into the 19th century, with visits to Civil War sites and majestic plantations.

One of the plantations, *Oak Alley,* lies close by the river, the entrance lined by 28 Virginia Oak trees that are 300 years old. It looked like *Gone With The Wind.* On one end of the oak-lined alley was the pillared mansion; and on the other, the tethered ship reminiscent of the play *ShowBoat.*

Amidst all that splendor, tragedy hit the plantation when the Master, Mr. Stafford died. In her mourning, Mrs. Stafford withdrew from all activities, moved out of the bedroom, and dressed in black for the rest of her life. An oil painting of her, a youthful beauty, hangs in testimony to her grief in a 13-foot high hallway.

That visit to Oak Alley got me thinking about the losses that people experience in life, and how we handle them.

I looked back on my own life, and realized that I had gone through many losses, not so different from everyone else I know who are the same age. Although the choice I made to retire from the priesthood was voluntary, nevertheless the loss I experienced has been surprising to me.

Then I lost my wife to cancer in 1981. For a while, I was a "Carol-haunted man." I am still reminded by dreams, or by unexpected situations, of both of these losses, which happened at different stages of my life. They are not completely "behind me."

If I let it, I can work up strong emotions about other losses as well as these two. A failed relationship, friends who have moved away or have died, termination of a job, financial security, etc.

Memories and emotional flashbacks appear unbidden, at the strangest times, to upset my serenity, my emotional stability.

People differ in the ways that they handle losses. Some, like Mrs. Stafford, get stuck in the past and become haunted by it, and never move on. It could be a deceased spouse. It could be a memory of abuse as a child, as portrayed in the movie *Affliction*. It could be a former marriage, or a difficult divorce. Some find it hard, if not impossible, to let go and move on.

Others are able to "put it behind them," i.e. suffer losses and move on. Sometimes I am surprised by how quickly and serenely people are able to leave behind some tragic event in their lives. A friend of mine who had lived into her 70's had a lifetime of illnesses, operations and family deaths. She was able to move on and not dwell on them. She remained active and social till the end, dressing "up" for every occasion to lift her spirits and enjoy as much of life as she could.

There are yet others who will hold on for a spell, and then make the effort to "let go." They will experience nostalgia, or periods of sadness. They may arrange anniversary memorials, as a means of not forgetting, but basically they will handle the losses and not allow the losses to take over.

Vincent B. Cardarelli, Th.M., CADC

Each one has his own personal style of experiencing grief.

Regardless, we go from one loss to another, one change to another, until as Judith Viorst says in one of her poems, we realize that a lot of time has passed while we were not paying attention.

> *What am I doing with a mid-life crisis?*
> *This morning I was seventeen.*
> *I have barely begun the beguine and it's*
> *Good-night ladies*
> *Already.*
> *While I've been wondering who to be*
> *When I grow up someday,*
> *My acne has vanished away and it's*
> *Sagging kneecaps*
> *Already.*
> *Why do I seem to remember Pearl Harbor?*
> *Surely I must be too young.*
> *When did the boys I once clung to*
> *Start losing their hair?*
> *Why can't I take barefoot walks in the park*
> *Without giving my kidneys a chill?*
> *There's poetry left in me still and it*
> *Doesn't seem fair.*
> *While I was thinking I was just a girl*
> *My future turned into my past.*
> *The time for wild kisses goes fast and it's*
> *Time for Sanka.*
> *Already?*

3. HANDLING LOSSES #2

Handling Losses Is a Key to Serenity

In her book, *Necessary Losses,* one of my favorite authors writes about "the loves, illusions, dependencies and impossible expectations that all of us have to give up in order to grow." It's a relatively easy book to read, witty and poetic, and I recommend it as a self-help book.

The message of the book is that some losses are necessary, i.e. no one can escape them since they are a part of life. Loss of the original "paradise" of the womb, when one is born; loss of childhood and innocence; loss of mother-love and family life; loss of friends and relatives by death; loss of health; loss of goals and dreams.

On the other hand, some losses are not necessary or inevitable, but are the result of choices that we make, like divorce, or leaving a job or retirement.

Then there are losses that are even more difficult to understand and accept—

those that result from the "fickle hand of fate." Some call it bad luck, or the Will of God, or whatever. These are events like accidents, illnesses, floods, etc. Such losses are certainly not necessary, but often they are the most traumatic to bear.

Finally, there are losses resulting from impossible expectations—expectations of what life or love can deliver for me. When I don't get what I expect, I experience disillusionment and a sense of loss—grief.

When loss occurs, my mind tells me that what was, is no longer; but my emotions don't go along with my head. I feel resistant; I can't accept it. It's like standing on a platform over a chasm, and someone pulls the platform out from under you. It's like an emptiness and a void, except it's not under your feet, it's in your abdomen and in your heart. Even though you know that what you lost is not there, and won't be, nevertheless you feel as if you are restlessly searching - searching for the lost object, casting about for a safe haven.

One way or the other, the greater majority of people handle losses in a healthy way. And thus the old saw: "Time heals all wounds." Briefly put, what it takes to handle loss is first to accept the reality—really accept it; and then, let it go. The process of separation is called mourning, or bereavement.

The process is somewhat alleviated if one is able to reach out, to friends to family, to other interests, etc. Sitting Shivah, visiting the sick and dying, are rituals that have developed because they help the grieving person to get started.

One needs to have perspective on his own life. Look back; count the losses, and then you will see that out of the loss came another opportunity, another aspect or phase of life. It was like the end of a chapter and the beginning of another; or like the life and death cycle of perennials.

Faith, or a belief system, like a theology, or philosophy, or a humanism which makes sense of what happens in life is a valuable tool in handling loss. We need to know intellectually and feel emotionally that what happens to us, especially the losses, has some overall meaning, fits into some greater plan, and is not for naught.

Sometimes we want to cry out: "Enough, already!" But, says Judith Viorst, "these losses are part of life...The road to human development is paved with renunciation. Throughout our life we grow by giving up. We give up some of our deepest attachments to others. We give up certain cherished parts of ourselves. We must confront, in the dreams we dream, as well as in our intimate relationships, all that we never will have and never will be. Passionate investment leaves us vulnerable to loss. And sometimes, no matter how clever we are, we must lose."

4. SERENITY AND THE SEPTEMBER OF MY YEARS

I'm not much for repetition, in the sense of getting into a rut and doing things the same way at the same time for long periods. But one of the habits I acquired was to listen to Frank Sinatra on the Sid Mark program on Sunday mornings on FM 96.5.

Today, I listened to a number of songs that referred to the older years. Sinatra, I think, really captured the feelings and experiences, as well as the longing and losses associated with the September of our years.

Some of his songs describe the struggle of living with unfulfilled dreams; some paint the joy of looking back on successes; but in all of them he does so with understanding and peaceful resignation. There is one entitled "The Single Man" that hits home.

He reflects a serenity in the songs that I would like to have at this stage of my life.

Whether he had it or not in his real life, I don't know. From afar, it seems that he had a roller-coaster existence, and it is hard to say whether that produced serenity or unease.

Secretly, I wanted to idolize him, but felt somewhat ashamed because of his notorious style of life. However, he does grasp the experience of getting older in his romantic and lyrical recordings.

In one, he laments the loss of youth and wants to hold on to it by doing the things that young people do, for example, find the "love of his life." In another he poignantly rhymes how lonely it is to be alone with the memories of lost love. And he tops it all off with *My Way*, looking back and being satisfied with it all.

Attempting to stave off the reality of age threatens serenity. But really, how does one get used to aging? It's not easy, but it's what one has to do. Speaking for myself, sometimes I am more comfortable than at other times with the piling on of years.

Some people find comfort in their grandchildren. Some find meaning in activities centered around senior centers; as I said, I haven't been able to stick to any one thing for long periods. (Maybe that's just an excuse for "holding on.") Terri, a classmate of mine living in Florida, goes to church-sponsored activities and is active in her senior center.

Dancing has kept me "young," and maybe that's why I like Sinatra; his rhythms are so easy to dance to.

Loneliness is a bug-a-boo. It lurks along the way; and as long as I am "doing" something then I can keep it in the shadows. But when I have long blocks of time with nothing to "do" then it rises up like bile after an upset stomach.

When grandchildren walk in, the look of happiness on grandma's face makes it all worthwhile. You can enjoy them for their own sakes, without the worry of having to discipline them. You can spoil them and it won't harm them.

Wisdom comes from the experience of having been "through it before," and that gives us the ability not "to sweat the little things."

One of the common concerns for the senior citizen is that of savings and assets. What do we do with it? Trusts? Spend it? Long term care? Is there any right answer to these questions? Some have many assets; some have few, and some have none. Maybe no one can tell you what to do, but one of the things NOT to do is to bury your head in the sand and postpone getting information pertinent to your own situation.

We would also like to leave some kind of testament behind...a memorial, as it were. A few years ago I recorded an auto-biographical account of my life and gave it to my daughter as a birthday gift. I can add to it as time goes on.

With all the technology available today, I'm sure you can come up with creative ways of doing the same thing.

One of Sinatra's ballads is "Let Me Try Again." You may be able to do that with a relationship, but you can't do it with your life. You pass this way only once; might as well enjoy it—so pray for serenity.

5. SERENITY AND SENIOR-I-TIS:

Reflecting on a Life in Progress

Senior-i-tis the condition of being preoccupied with aging, with the title of Senior Citizen. I hope it is temporary, because suddenly I find myself confronted not only with the beginning of a new millennium but also with the beginning of my eighth decade of life.

It's hard to believe that I have been around that long. I don't feel that old. "You don't look that old." Yeah, right!

I have kept a journal for the past 30 years, and as I write my thoughts and feelings about my awareness of the passing years, I wonder whether others have similar reactions.

They say that with age comes wisdom. When I ask myself what have I learned that qualifies as wisdom, the answer is that some things I have learned and some things I have not. My journal proves it. Reading over my past entries, I see that in certain situations, I have made the same mistakes over and over, without ever mastering them. That does not qualify as being "wise."

Some things I have learned, however. Like not taking myself too seriously, and learning to laugh at myself when I make mistakes. Like not being so defensive when someone points out some foible, or some error.

Vincent B. Cardarelli, Th.M., CADC

I have learned to be more aware of my emotions, and to be more in control of them, rather than be led around by the nose by a passing feeling. Well, OK, not *all* the time.

I have learned that I don't have to be a "parent" any more; my children now know more than I and in some ways can tell me what to do. The torch has been passed! They are now the parents and have to worry instead of me. So I can just relax and enjoy being a "father" and a grandfather. Maybe I have acquired some wisdom after all.

Something else I realize: Years ago, as I was planning my future and going through the experiences of career choice, marriage, buying a house, having children, job changes, etc., I wasn't so sure about what I was doing, whether it was the right thing or not. But now, as I look back it seems as if someone had written the script and that I knew what I was doing all along. I'm sure about it now.

Let me tell you, though, one trait dies hard: the need to be right. It's hard to say to another, "You may be right." Sometimes I want desperately to be heard, or to win an argument, or to prove my point. Sometimes I can get carried away about it. Yet when I am able to let the other person have his way, I walk away quiet, composed and serene.

My serenity is in jeopardy when I begin to feel lonely. I've been alone for most of my life, and I don't need anyone to do either the "traditional" men's or women's work.

I can handle that. What I don't handle too well is the loneliness that creeps in from time to time. That's when I get frantic and wish for a quick fix, like a Glinda, the Good Witch, (in the guise of a wife.)

I also get rattled by the prospect of non-existence. You know—will I be around after death? Will I be aware of me and my family then as I am now? Will the tapestry of my history fade in one or two generations, or will I carry into eternity a photo album of the many wonderful people and experiences I have encountered? I used to have all the answers when I was younger (the soul lives on until the resurrection, etc.) but now I have this vague insecurity about all of that.

Although I plan to be around for a long time, and although I still have many things to accomplish, I know that in the end, my life will be essentially unfinished. I would like to come to terms with that.

Willy Russell, author of the play *Shirley Valentine*, said: "There's a line in a Paul Simon song that goes, 'The thought that life could be better is woven into our hearts, and our bones.' That's our blessing. And in a way, it's our curse, too."

6. GEE, I'M TERRIBLY SORRY, BUT I'M DRAWING A BLANK

The story is told of two couples leaving a restaurant after dinner. The two men are walking in front of the two wives. Jim is telling Al about a dinner that he and his wife had the night before and really praising it for the food and ambiance.

Al asks what the name of the restaurant is.

Jim says: "The name is...uh, what's the name of that flower that is red and has a long stem with thorns on it?" Al says: "You mean a 'rose'?" Jim says, "Yeah, that's it..." then turns to his wife and says: "Rose, what's the name of that restaurant that we went to last night?"

I'm often in a conversation where I can't pull up some word or name. I say, "Gee, I'm drawing a blank." It's almost as if my memory disk is slow on the draw, and I know that I have the fact in storage, but like a frozen computer, it's not coming up on the screen of my brain.

Last week, I took down directions to go to a Rescue Station to look at some dogs for a possible adoption. I'm pretty good at directions and rarely get lost. So I confidently got in the car, backed down the driveway, and drove off. On the way, I "remembered" that I forgot to take along the written directions.

TOWARD SERENITY

Friends have told me that I am distracted, that I don't pay attention, that I am getting older, etc. But the fact that my memory misfires is not new. In high school, history was my worse subject, because I had to remember facts and names and dates.

When I crammed, I was OK, but ask me something while I was on my feet in class and I would often draw a blank. I just couldn't remember who it was that wanted to put Napoleon in a cage, or what year the Hapsburgs ruled Austria-Hungary.

I do a lot reading, and often quote pearls of wisdom taken from the books I have read. But when I go to the library to borrow another book, I forget which ones I have already read.

Phone numbers I easily recall; peoples' names I don't.

I am constantly saying to friends that I meet at the A&P or on the street: "Help me out. I don't remember your name. I'm drawing a blank."

I'm older, yes. But I remember my father chiding me when I was young. He, of course, had a prodigious memory, and could recite the Psalms of the Old Testament verbatim. He never lost that memory.

Some explain the loss of memory by "selective attention (or inattention)." Others by having recourse to some gene activity regulating long-term memory. Sure, there is the reality of some pathology such as Alzheimer's that can cause memory disruption. But we're not talking about that in this chapter.

My daughter alternately gets a big kick out of, or gets irritated with, my memory lapses. And really, sometimes it is comical, e.g., when I sound like Norm Crosby, or Mrs. Malaprop, who are prime examples of this sort of slip of tongue or memory.

For years, I berated myself because I wasn't on the ball. I feel great when I can remember someone's name. It's a compliment to that person. But often I'd meet a friend in the most unexpected of places, e.g. the Colosseum in Rome,

Vincent B. Cardarelli, Th.M., CADC

struggle unsuccessfully to recall the name, and beg his pardon. Sure, their names would pop up later—in the shower or when talking about the veal cacciatore at dinner. But the harm was already done and the opportunity gone.

I have achieved some kind of serenity in the past few years, even though I have never gotten to the root of my problem, much less solved it. I just live with it, and don't consider it a "problem" anymore.

I now know that the important things I will remember (at least most of the time), and so I don't try to clutter up my mind with a lot of facts, dates, trivia, which, if I force myself or train myself by self-help books or attending conferences on how to enhance my memory, even though there are others who bedazzle me with their computerized memory... Geez, I forgot what I was going to say!

Well, I'm sure there's always someone around like my daughter who will remind me. So, why worry about it?

7. CHRONICALLY ILL

Living With Chronically Ill People

Those of you who live with a chronically ill person—this chapter is for you. If you live with a loved one who has Alzheimer's disease, asthma, alcoholism, eating disorders or other disabling illness, I ask you to heed what is written here.

"You"—as a significant other—can be an adult or a child, a spouse or family member, a lover or a parent. If you have been caring for another for any length of time, you can be suffering from some symptoms of your own, and sometimes they can be quite serious.

Joe Kellerman, author of "Family of the Alcoholic," said it best when he wrote: "First, the family member makes an adjustment to the illness; then, when that no longer works, he makes a re-adjustment, then makes yet another re-adjustment, and, finally, he becomes maladjusted." That description applies to many caretakers.

The caretaker tries to control unnatural behavior of the sick person by so many adjustments and changes in her own behavior that, after a while, she herself becomes ill.

By trying to help the chronically ill person, the significant other often becomes depressed, resentful or anxiety-ridden. It is common for the significant other to have recourse to a therapist, who usually counsels him or her to "take care of yourself" by planning time away from the patient, by getting a hobby to occupy down time, or by taking a vacation. You, the caretaker, may be counseled to get a visiting nurse, go to a self-help group—and even to a lawyer for legal advice. But, in many cases, these avenues of help are not practical, because chronic illnesses are not debilitating enough to command alternate funding or assistance from outside agencies.

When the situation becomes too stressful, you may seek relief by temporary outside help from family, or short hospitalization, but these solutions are not effective to relieve the underlying stress.

One family member said to me: "As long as I don't see her, I am O.K., but when I see her or talk with her, then I lose it."

It sounds selfish and uncaring to be told to "take care of yourself." But in reality, it is just the opposite. When a child is involved in a family where there is a chronically ill person, then the situation is especially poignant. In such a family, the adults can remember back when the patient was healthy and functioning well. But children don't know any better. They have nothing to compare it to. A child who has learned only maladaptive behavior will experience a "funny feeling" when invited to behave in a normal, healthy manner by "taking care of himself." The child can't remember a time when it was better and he was able to act without worrying about the sick person.

Such a child, when he/she grows up, may, in fact, choose maladjusted friends with whom he/she feels "comfortable." That is "normal" for them. They relate to peers about whom parents and teachers warn that such friends are not good for them.

Sometimes life itself will act as a teacher to a growing child; or maybe the right kind of help will appear at the right time, to redirect the child. Either way, the child needs to learn that he or she has a right to what is normal, even if it may seem strange. The child needs to be affirmed and reaffirmed as an important person, worthwhile and entitled to having his own needs met.

The same is true of an adult who has the obligation of a chronically ill loved one; namely, that certain needs have to be met in order to feel and act normal. Sacrifice is needed to take care of another, but setting some limits is also needed. A balance of the two is the goal. A therapist's practice includes "caretakers" who have been so preoccupied by the care of the chronically ill relative that they have denied themselves their own needs. As a result, they have become maladjusted themselves.

A 16-year old son whose mother cared for an alcoholic spouse wrote me a letter and described his mother as being so angry and demanding that no matter what he did for her, he couldn't seem to please her.

Taking care of oneself means more than vacations and social agencies; it means literally to be healthy in the face of others' illness. It is a difficult task, and it is made more difficult because doing so does not come naturally; it needs to be practiced.

Knowing how to set limits on *oneself* is a basic skill to rehearse; caretakers, by nature, are primed to take care of others first, and allow themselves to go beyond reasonable limits.

Sometimes the best help we can give to others is to help ourselves.

Section VI—Alcohol and Drugs

1. ALCOHOLISM #1

Serenity and Our Attitudes Toward Drinking

The Serenity Prayer goes like this: "God grant me the serenity to accept the things I cannot change, the courage to change the things I can and the wisdom to know the difference." It is not only the basis for the book, but also a guide for your decisions about the use of alcohol.

The use of alcohol affects our lives—for good and for ill; and the way we view alcohol contributes to how we use it. The aim of this chapter is to understand our attitudes about drinking habits and secondly, to avoid a simplistic—a black or white, right or wrong—approach to the topic. Some people hardly use alcohol at all; others are only social drinkers; others are "problem drinkers;" and a small but significant number are 'alcoholics." This chapter deals with "problem drinking."

Alcohol is neither all good nor all bad. I—you—need to make choices about how we use it. How much should I drink? How much is too much for me? Am I in control of alcohol or is it in control of me?

My serenity depends on a wise choice, and for some, alcohol is an enticing substitute for serenity.

Alcohol makes us feel good; that's called euphoria. Alcohol is a social lubricant; it enhances a good meal; it is a means of celebration at games, rites of passage, family gatherings, and rituals. Bread and wine have been staples of human existence.

Many see it as an evil and call its use a sin. Many have seen it as a crime, and tried to prohibit it legally. Neither simplistic, absolutist approach has worked.

How can you proscribe what the Bible calls "a gift of God that gladdens the heart of man" (and woman).

Total abstinence is also an absolutist approach that counselors have used in the treatment of overdrinking. Both AA and treatment programs insist that abstinence is the only solution that is effective. Again this is an all or nothing solution.

Abstinence is definitely the only method that works for an "alcoholic," i.e., one who suffers from the disease of alcoholism (called *Alcohol Dependence.*) But it is not acceptable for a great number of drinkers, especially young adults. And it is not acceptable for millions of social drinkers, who do not have a problem with alcohol.

However, there are in our country millions of people who are "problem drinkers," that is, people who are not alcoholics, per se, but certainly abuse alcohol. The campus week-end bingers, the high-school students who use inappropriately. It may be true that abstinence is not for them, but it is also true that they can't be nonchalant and reckless about their drinking habits.

Misuse of alcohol causes anxiety, depression, violence and a number of other social ills for a significant number of Americans. My guess is that more employees lose their jobs because of alcohol abuse than because of down-sizing. Every year 1.5 million drivers are stopped for DUI—35,000 to 40,000 in New Jersey alone.

"Briefly put, problem drinkers are people who have had problems because of drinking—a DUI arrest, marital discord, showing up late for work, getting into a fight. But they don't drink steadily and don't go through withdrawal when they stop." (U.S. News, Sept. 1997) Their calling card is

"I am not an alcoholic," and they may be correct. But they are problem drinkers, because they misuse alcohol.

"Misuse of alcohol costs the nation dearly — $100 billion a year in quantifiable costs, in addition to untold emotional pain. These costs are incurred...by problem drinkers who are four times more numerous than alcoholics, are more active in society, and usually reject abstinence as a solution. Alcohol figures in 41 percent of traffic crash fatalities and is a factor in 50 percent of homicides, 30 percent of suicides, and 30 percent of accidental deaths," says the same News article. Periodically, we read of a college student who drinks himself to death at a frat party.

"Heavy drinking also increases the risk of cancer, heart disease, and stroke, long before people have to worry about cirrhosis of the liver, brain damage or other skid-row ailments." Problem drinking is not alcoholism, but the toll of problem drinking is far greater than the toll of alcoholism.

There are about 160 million drinkers—occasional, social, problem, alcoholic—in the U.S.A. Estimates (they vary a lot) are that 20 percent of these have a "problem" with alcohol. That adds up to about 32 million adults (give or take a few million.) Five percent are 'alcoholic," about 8 million (give or take a few million). But no matter how you look at it, there are a lot of people who are adversely affected by overdrinking.

Granted, "alcoholics" cannot drink at all—one drink will ultimately lead to more, etc. (See next chapter). But we do have to find other solutions that are workable and acceptable, solutions that are medical and practical for the problem drinkers.

"The majority of people who drink heavily do not become alcoholics...and the majority of people who cut back or quit drinking do so on their own. Many of those people binge drank in their 20's at college parties, at after-work happy hours, or during Sunday afternoon football games, then got a good job, got married, got busy, and lost interest

Vincent B. Cardarelli, Th.M., CADC

in getting smashed. In the researchers' lingo, they "matured out." (U.S.News)

Remedy magazine recently reported on a study by physician Michael F. Fleming. The study showed that "even a brief discussion with a physician can help problem drinking. Over the years, the focus has been on severe alcoholism not problem drinking—yet problem drinking affects about three times more people and causes most of the alcohol-related accidents and abuse in the U.S."

He says that many patients, as well as a good number of their doctors are unaware that they drink potentially harmful amounts.

So: How much should I drink? How much is too much? Am I in control of my drinking? Check out the accompanying chart.

Abstinent (or almost)		Low-Risk		Problem		Alcoholic	
40%		35%		20%		5%	
Men	*Women*	*Men*	*Women*	*Men*	*Women*	*Men*	*Women*
Less than one drink per month	Less than one drink per month	Fewer than 8 drinks per week	Fewer than 8 drinks per week	15 or more drinks per week or 5 or more at a time	8 or more drinks per week or 4 or more at a time	So dependent on alcohol that drinking leads to severe consequences	

2. ALCOHOLISM #2

An Alcoholic's Irresponsibility Affects the Whole Family

A *problem drinker* is one who has problems because of drinking: a DUI arrest, marital discord, showing up late for work, etc. They don't have the classic symptoms of *Alcoholism,* such as withdrawal when they stop.

This chapter focuses on the *illness* of Alcoholism. An "alcoholic" is a person who is alcohol-dependent, the proper medical term. That is, the person progressively develops a dependency on alcohol. An alcoholic is one who shows at least three of the following symptoms:

1. **Tolerance.** He/she can drink more and more and show it less and less. However, after time, the alcoholic loses tolerance, and once he starts, cannot stop until he reaches the buzz he needs to feel "normal."

2. **Withdrawal.** When an alcoholic tries to stop, he experiences withdrawal symptoms that vary from the shakes to a very severe and dangerous seizure, which can be lethal.

3. **An inability to cut down.** This is usually described as a loss of control. There comes with the progression of the illness a **craving**, an urge, which is compulsive and is a hallmark of the "illness."

4. **Sacrificing work, family or social events to drink.** It almost seems that alcohol acts like a mistress, and as such is a real threat to marriage, job and friends.

5. **Devoting a lot of time to finding and consuming alcohol.** This is usually called "preoccupation with alcohol."

6. **Persistence in drinking despite related health problem.** Problems like emphysema, cancer, high blood pressure, depression, anxiety and a variety of vague undiagnosable complaints.

7. **Continuing to drink despite the recurrence of increasingly severe crises.**

8. **GUILT.** He/she hides bottles, creates an alibi system explaining "why" he drinks, and lies about the amount.

The determining factor for a problem drinker is—how much do you drink. But for an alcoholic it is not how much do you drink but—what it does to you when you DO drink, no matter what the amount.

"*Alcoholism* per se cannot be blamed for the majority of social ills linked to drinking in this country," reports U.S. News. Overdrinking, or misuse of alcohol, is what costs the nation so much.

But *alcoholism does affect the family—and everyone in the family*. I'll save for the next chapter the effects on the family. But note well, that spouses, children, as well as lovers, friends and co-workers are impacted by the irresponsible behavior of the alcoholic.

And that is the operative word: irresponsibility. Since the illness is one of dependency, the alcoholic will slowly, but inevitably become lax in his duties, and then someone else—usually the spouse—will "take over" and become what has been termed the "codependent." The alcoholic becomes dependent on alcohol; the spouse or significant other becomes dependent on the irresponsible behavior of the alcoholic. It's inevitable. The alcoholic is afflicted, the family is affected.

The problem drinker (not yet dependent) usually has control over the frequency and amount of his drinking, and most often can learn to drink socially with minimal intervention. But the alcoholic as well as his family usually need treatment to recover from the illness and its effects. That may seem like bad news, But the good news is that the treatment works and families do recover. From dysfunctional, they become weller-than-well.

Alcoholism is a fatal illness, but it is the most hopeful of all fatal illnesses.

Here's a short (not infallible) test to take to determine whether one may be alcoholic; it's called the **CAGE** test.

- Have you ever felt that you should **Cut** down on your drinking?
- Have people **Annoyed** you by criticizing your drinking?
- Have you ever felt bad or **Guilty** about your drinking?
- Have you ever had a drink first thing in the morning to steady your nerves or to get rid of a hangover (**Eye-opener**)?

Two or more **yes** responses shows a potential for dependency.

3. ALCOHOLISM #3

Children of Alcoholics and Serenity

For every person who is afflicted with Alcoholism, several others are *affected*. The spouse is the primary victim, as is discussed in other chapters. The children of alcoholics are also often affected.

The decade of the '70's produced a sea of literature on children of alcoholics. Numerous clinical experts wrote and spoke of the issue, and the good news was that we became aware of the millions of children who lived with alcohol problems and alcoholism. The bad news, however, was that a lot of what was publicized was speculation and overgeneralization.

Books, videos, and conferences dealt with topics like the roles that children learn in the family, characteristics of children of alcoholics, codependency, etc.

Subsequent research has shown that although the observations of the clinicians were accurate in a significant number of children of alcoholics, the majority of children grew up healthy and relatively unaffected by parental addiction.

The research also shows, however, that for those children who *are* affected, certain specific problems surface during the four phases of development.

During pregnancy, it is 1) Fetal Alcohol Syndrome (FAS) and 2) Fetal Alcohol Effect (FAE). FAS is a constellation of physical and intellectual disabilities that are a direct result of the mother's drinking during pregnancy. It is observable immediately after birth.

FAE surfaces during early childhood. Fetal Alcohol Effect is the term for several symptoms that are less observable and less severe than FAS, but affects numerically more children. The symptoms are hyperactivity, inability to pay attention, learning disabilities and poor impulse control. It is sometimes diagnosed as Attention Deficit Disorder (ADD).

The scary part of FAE is that there is some evidence that even the father can transmit this disorder through alcohol-affected genes.

During the phase of adolescence, emotional problems surface, including anxiety and depression and the more serious conduct disorder. It's at this time that adolescents learn to medicate their problems by using alcohol or drugs. Because of that, "children of alcoholics are more prone to become alcoholics."

During both adolescence and adulthood, there is a four-times greater chance that children of alcoholics will develop a dependence on alcohol and/or drugs

Also during adulthood, some COA's overcompensate by becoming high achievers, others will become caretakers both in their families as well as in their careers; these latter become teachers, doctors, nurses and social workers. That can be both good and bad: good because they contribute to society; bad because they have a tendency to be unhappy in their choice of work.

Research now shows that alcoholism by itself is not a guarantee that children will inherit the illness, but when there coexist in the parents some other identifiable risk factors, especially anti-social personality, then the chances are greater that the COA's will develop behavioral and

Vincent B. Cardarelli, Th.M., CADC

emotional problems and a dependency on alcohol and drugs.

Although living with problem drinking or alcoholism may not automatically cause severe problems for COA's, it will certainly affect their serenity—the ability to live peacefully and without anxiety.

The "cost" of overdrinking not only spirals upward of billions of dollars in this country, but the cost in terms of serenity is also expensive.

Our attitude toward alcohol ought to be: proper use of alcohol adds to our enjoyment of life; but misuse and abuse of alcohol sabotages our pursuit of happiness and causes a lot of anxiety.

For further information, contact the National Association For Children of Alcoholics. Call 1-800-554-COAS, toll-free.

4. CO-DEPENDENCY:

The Obsessive Caretaker

I started working in the field of Alcoholism in 1972 when I was asked to lead a group of spouses of alcoholics who were being treated for their illness. It was one of the first treatment programs anywhere for spouses and families of alcoholics.

That was my first experience with "codependents." At the time, they were called "co-alcoholics" or "near-alcoholics." Many of them, mostly women, seemed extremely resentful, angry and "bitchy." As I got to know them, I found that these "caretakers"—codependents—were really loving and caring people. But they had lost their own identity by obsessively caring for the alcoholic, and as a result were suffering themselves.

In the early '80's the term "codependent" became popular to describe the spouses of alcoholics and chemically dependent people. The word comes from the fact that just as the alcoholic becomes dependent on alcohol, so the spouse (or family member) becomes dependent, hence "co-dependent" on the behavior of the alcoholic.

It is a fact that Alcoholism is an illness of Dependency, a compulsive, addicting kind of Dependency. Untreated it leads to divorce, desertion, death, incarceration or insanity...for all affected.

Melody Beattie defines a codependent person as one who has "let another person's behavior affect him/her, and who is obsessed with controlling that person's behavior."

It is clear that alcoholism fosters codependency because a family member must interact with an important person in his life who has a serious illness. And that illness causes erratic behavior and ever increasing demands and needs. That kind of behavior over a period of time is "crazy-making"—you can't live as if it didn't exist; a caring person will automatically react to it.

Let me insert here that other kinds of families can also cause codependency. Families that have strict rules, and families that have silent rules have an extremely powerful influence, especially on the children. Silent rules prohibit open discussion, about problems, feelings, or relationships. Silent rules place high expectations (perfectionism) on children to perform and they prohibit a playful and fun-loving approach to life. Take a moment and list for yourself some of the "rules" in your own family and see how they still affect your behavior. For example, parents who tell their children that they "shouldn't feel like that..." are operating on the silent rule of "Do not talk openly about your negative feelings."

But back to the main point: When you live with a person who is dependent on alcohol (or a drug), you must put yourself in second place in order to continue to live with that person. You are forced to react to the other person's needs, and a pattern of behavior (codependency) develops which is just a compulsive as the addiction itself.

And it is just as difficult to change the pattern and recover. The "other person" may be a child, spouse, lover, friend, sibling, parent or even a co-worker.

After a while the codependent becomes a caretaker to the extreme of taking over the responsibility of the alcoholic and trying to control his life. The codependent reacts to what he perceives are the problems, needs, pains of the other. It's natural to want to help others, but a codependent does so compulsively; that is, he or she is not free to say "no" to the needs of other when they are in conflict with his own.

As a result, the co-dependent co-alcoholic, after having repeatedly "re-adjusted" her own behavior, becomes "maladjusted" herself. The axiom is: "It is impossible to live in a normal fashion with an active alcoholic." The co-dependent's own life has become unmanageable.

I'd like to suggest an exercise for you if you think that someone in your family abuses alcohol or drugs. The aim of the following questions is to make you aware of how your life is not your own, and how powerless you are over your loved one and over his or her behavior.

Even though you have tried everything to control him/her, it hasn't worked. Not only has it not worked, but your own life has become unmanageable. As one woman put it: "I have been exiled from myself without even suspecting it."

Take a sheet of paper and list each question, leaving a space so you can write down your thoughts and reactions. Follow it up by examples for each of the questions.

1) In what ways have I been preoccupied with the alcohol (drug user)? E.g. I could not go to sleep because I was worrying.
2) In what ways have I attempted unsuccessfully to control the use of alcohol? E.g. by nagging, setting up rules and guidelines.
3) In what ways have I punished the alcoholic for his behavior? E.g. giving him the silent treatment, or refusing affection.
4) In what ways have I covered up problems, or minimized his behavior? E.g. making up excuses for employer or teacher.

5) In what ways have I lost control of myself? E.g. by carrying resentments, fears, panic attacks, or flying off the handle.
6) How have I blamed the alcoholic for my own unmanageability? E.g. by resorting to "If only you..."

What do your answers tell you? Hopefully, you will become aware of how you yourself have been affected by the illness. You really can't do anything about your own misery until you do become aware of your own behavior, and how unmanageable it has become.

That is the first step.

Karen Horney wrote:

"Until now I have known nothing, understood nothing, and as a result could love nothing, for the simple, unbelievable reason that I wasn't here! For over 40 years, I have been exiled from myself without even suspecting it. Merely to understand this, now, is tremendous. It is not only the end of all that dying, it is to begin life."

5. RECOVERY FROM CODEPENDENCY

It bears repetition that codependency means obsessive and compulsive caretaking.

Much of what we do is on behalf of others; however, codependency is "other-oriented" behavior that is carried to the extreme.

Codependency does not apply to the charitable actions that we take on behalf of family, friends, co-workers, and the disabled; these actions may look the same, but the motivation is different—one is charitable, and the other is compulsive—and the amount of gratification is different. Charitable work makes one happy; codependent work makes one resentful. Charitable work is gratuitous; codependent work is instinctual and impulse-driven.

Those who live with alcoholics and drug-users are constrained; in a sense, they're forced to be codependent. There is what is called the "slippery slope" down which the caretaker slides. First the caretaker adjusts to the behavior of the alcoholic; then after a while she has to readjust; that is followed yet again by another re-adjustment; and that is followed by a MAL-adjustment. By that time, the co-alcoholic becomes "sick" herself.

That is the time for *recovery*. To recover self-esteem, to get rid of the resentments, to become more assertive and more "one's own person"—is to recover.

Let me debunk the advice that divorce is the only way to recover from codependency—"Get rid of the bum." If that is the first step, then chances are the codependent will seek out yet another dependent person "to help."

There is one *condition,* and three *steps* that lead to recovery. The **condition** is that the codependent must **detach.** Detachment is a condition because since the CD's behavior is compulsive, the only way to learn new behavior is to stop the old knee-jerk reaction of running to another's plight. To detach means that the CD pays attention to what is happening, but does not allow himself to get emotionally involved. Let me tell you that learning to do this is very difficult. It is pretty hard when confronted with the police who are bringing home your husband to say "Oh." And not to get in there and question and explain etc. You don't run away, and you don't get all sarcastic. You just pay attention—and (at least for the present) do nothing. You don't ignore, on the one hand, and you don't jump in on the other. In other words, you don't react.

After one is able to detach, then the **first *step*** is to become aware of ones' own actions, and how easily a CD can be sucked into caretaking behavior. To her it looks like she is showing loving care; to an other it looks like she is a controlling person. She needs to become aware, without judging. Here is where Alanon, counseling, and literature can help. There's a web-site *www.gettingthemsober.com* that is very helpful.

The **second *step*** is to practice *entitlement.* After becoming aware of the tendency to take care of others and how pervasive it is, the CD must learn to feel and act as if she has a right to take care of herself first—at least some of the time. I am "entitled." I don't need permission to make myself happy, to make my own decisions; I don't need to feel like a criminal if I say "no" to some request or demand that is made of me.

TOWARD SERENITY

The "stuff" of recovery and healing is a gentle affirmation of self. You need to replace negative messages—"I'm not OK..." with positive messages. "I'm OK"

"I can't do it," with "I can do it." "I'm not entitled" with "I am entitled." The goal is self-esteem.

The **third** *step* is to be responsible for oneself. The other side of that coin is to allow the alcoholic to be responsible for himself. In the name of love, the CD tries to carry the weight of another's self-esteem as well as the burden of her own. It doesn't work; each must be responsible for him/her self.

The central message of this chapter is that a balance between taking care of oneself and taking care of others is the ideal for mental health and serenity. To recover from codependency does not mean *me first and the heck with others;* nor does it mean *you first and the heck with me.* It means the ability to go back and forth between care of self and care of others, and having the wisdom and the freedom to know which to choose.

You have a right to be a real person, one who enjoys a more authentic life. In order to do so, you need to take the first step of becoming aware, and then taking action.

6. STUDY ON BINGE DRINKING PROVES WHAT WE ALREADY KNOW

All the newspapers reported the results of a recent study on the effects of binge drinking by a pregnant woman on the brain of her unborn child.

"Although experiments in the study were conducted on laboratory rats," says the article, "experts said the findings offer an explanation of why children born to drinking mothers can suffer learning disabilities and other brain disorders." (Courier News, 2/11/00)

The study is startling and scary, because what it proves is that at a period "when developing brain cells are furiously building the connections needed for memory, learning and thought" the presence of alcohol causes neurological damage to the brain of the fetus.

"During this brain growth spurt...a single prolonged contact with alcohol—lasting for four hours or more—is enough to kill vast numbers of brain cells...The cells die by the millions and millions," says Dr. John W. Olney, one of the authors of the study.

The study, as well as the articles appearing in the papers, go on to conclude that "drinking in late pregnancy is really unsafe for the brain." That seems like common sense, and so obvious that it would prevent many mothers-to-be from using alcohol. But not so.

We really do not know how many children are born with the kind of brain damage described in this study. It is called Fetal Alcohol Effect (FAE), and it is not as noticeable as "Fetal Alcohol Syndrome" (FAS) which is a more serious disability, and is the result of prolonged drinking during gestation. One in 1000 babies is born with FAS. FAE is far more prevalent.

Since the brain continues to develop for a few years after birth, there should also be concern about giving any kind of drugs, even anesthesia for surgery, to children under the age of 2.

I've taken the occasion of the publication of this study to include this chapter because it certainly does have an effect on serenity. After almost 30 years working with alcoholics and their families, I can attest to the anxiety, pain and suffering that comes from abuse and dependence on alcohol (as well as other drugs.)

Recently, I talked with a psychopharmacologist who is an expert in working with alcoholics and their families. He said that it is not scientifically proven as a fact, but he believes that even when *fathers* are drinkers and conceive a child, it is possible for him to pass on some genetic damage. The drinking father, whose own genes are affected by prolonged drinking, does not usually pass on gross damage, but the kind of damage that is indicated in this study— namely, learning disabilities, impulse-driven behaviors, and poor attention span can be passed on.

I have often wondered how many ADD and ADHD diagnosed children are really children of alcoholics (mothers or fathers).

As scary as it is, however, there is good news. I have also been in the business long enough to see families many years later. These children grow up, they "catch up to themselves" and mature. It seems that other parts of the brain begin to do the work that the damaged part was unable to do in earlier years.

Vincent B. Cardarelli, Th.M., CADC

As long as these children do not turn to alcohol—or any other drug—to cope with their anxieties in adolescence, they will blossom and do well in life. I can't point to a study to prove this; it is my own observation and my own belief in the resilience of human nature.

It is a beautiful thing to watch a child who had difficulty in growing up, struggle through school, find his/her niche, and finally succeed in adulthood against all the dire predictions of the prognosticators who worked with the child early on.

I'm not a teetotaler. My family has had wine at table all of my life, and like the Bible says: Wine is a gift of God that gladdens the heart of man. For most people it is just that. But for some, it can be a disaster. We make a big mistake to underestimate the power and insidious nature of alcohol and drugs. The answer is to be aware.

7. BINGE DRINKING IS GETTING THE ATTENTION IT DESERVES.

I've been certified as an Alcoholism and Drug Counselor since 1978. I'm often asked by a client whether or not I am an alcoholic. I usually tell them to wait until we are finished with therapy before I answer that question. Interestingly, no one does ask at the end, because I guess they come to realize that since I understand addiction, it doesn't make any difference either way.

The percentage of people who are "alcoholic," i.e. diagnosable as such, is much smaller than the number of people who binge drink. *Alcoholism* is an illness; binge drinking is a social evil.

My own personal belief is that drinking in itself is not bad or good; it takes its place with many other pleasurable foods and drinks. Good thing that it was not discovered in the past 50 years; it would have been called a CDS, a controlled dangerous substance, and regulated like other prescription drugs.

The majority of people of every nation, men and women, drink socially and culturally.

As part of their recreation and as part of their heritage, alcohol—wine, beer, and liquor—is an integral part of their everyday life and rituals.

Vincent B. Cardarelli, Th.M., CADC

It is a fact that most people handle alcohol the way they handle other food and drink; that is, they handle it in a responsible and balanced way. Most people do not misuse it.

You don't normally see anyone eat "two six-packs" of bananas. Or a gallon of ice-cream. Or anything else.

When someone "binges," he/she usually has a problem with the item in question: sugar, cigarettes, alcohol, drugs, etc. Binge-ing behavior is usually a symptom of an underlying problem. OR—if the binge behavior is not caused by a problem, then the binge behavior will cause its own problems.

And that is the case on high school and college campuses. National attention is being focused on the binge-drinking by young adults.

Recently a consortium of college administrators issued a statement to the effect that binge-drinking on college campuses is a serious problem and is out of hand. In the statement they indicate that they plan "to discourage" the ubiquitous practice.

That is heartening news. No one can diagnose a high school student or a college age student as definitely being an alcoholic. It's too early. But it is definitely not too early to intervene in a lethal practice that has become almost an epidemic.

So much of the social and cultural activities of young people are centered around drinking. I don't think we can go back to prohibition-type control, even of under-age people. But **binge**-drinking is another matter entirely!

To binge means to get carried away; to do something in excess. To binge on alcohol means to drink too much by anyone's standards.

There are those who think one drink is too much. And then there are others who believe that there should be no limits. Let each person decide for himself.

But to drink to the point of getting blotto; to the point of blacking out (i.e. not have any memory of what happened);

to the point of becoming violent, or a danger to oneself or others—to drink to **that** point is too much no matter how many drinks one takes.

That, dear readers, is what a significant number of young people are doing. And finally someone who matters has noticed and tried to do something about it. And the truly exciting thing is that something is being done on a *public policy level.* This is not just an effort to instruct students in the classroom about the evils of drinking.

Surveys and studies have now "proven" what we knew all along by observation alone—namely, that binge drinking is a real problem for young adults between the ages of 14 and 22, whether they go to school or not.

It's futile to try to determine whether someone at 18 or 20 is an alcoholic or not; you'll get an argument on both sides of the question.

But when an underage driver causes a death (his own or others), or when a young adult commits suicide (a major cause of premature death), or when one overdoses because of poor judgment, or when date rape occurs, most often under the influence, or when a young person steals a car on a dare, or breaks and enters under peer pressure—when any of these things happen under the influence of alcohol or drugs, it is of no help whatsoever to know whether or not the person is an "alcoholic."

The statistics show that 80% or more of the damage—deaths, violence, rapes etc—is the result of **too much** drinking, not 'alcoholic" drinking. Binge drinking is a social and cultural problem, and it needs to be addressed on that level.

So it is really good news to read that school administrators have resolved to band together and devise ways to lessen the phenomenon of binge-drinking.

Straight-laced administrators raised their eyebrows at the panty-raids of the post-war era. Libertarian administrators need to raise the red flag at the practice of binge-drinking.

Vincent B. Cardarelli, Th.M., CADC

It provides a measure of serenity to those of us who work with young people that something is being done to control these excesses.

8. ON THE USE OF MEDICATION TO ATTAIN SERENITY

As we progress in our knowledge of health and sickness, we have discovered not only new illnesses, but also new ways of treating them. Not only is this true for physical illnesses and trauma to the body, but it is also true for mental and emotional illnesses and disorders.

In the recent past few years, new medications have been marketed for the alleviation of suffering caused by mood disorders such as depression and anxiety, compulsive disorders such as alcoholism and other addictions, and by mental dysfunction, such as schizophrenia. In fact, the discovery and use of these new medications has effectively emptied out the psychiatric hospitals that used to lock up and restrain the mentally ill. They have been mainstreamed, for the most part, and are monitored by psychiatrists and out-patient clinics.

Most of a therapist's practice nowadays consists of clients who need support, or direction in coping with trauma, or help in making life decisions. Many are having a relationship problem. These types of emotionally charged situations do not usually need medication.

Professionals offer various modalities of therapy: insight or cognitive therapy; rational-emotive therapy;

Vincent B. Cardarelli, Th.M., CADC

behavior modification; hypnosis; conjoint or couple therapy. These are usually effective and produce the desired results.

However, there is a certain percentage of clients who will not respond to a helping hand or psychological intervention. Some will need medication either to get them unstuck, or to get control of runaway emotions. Some will need meds to maintain equilibrium.

When it comes to the use of medications for emotional problems, there are extremist/absolutist on both sides of the question. Some say that all problems are biological and so medication should be used to the exclusion of therapy. And on the opposite side, some say that no medication should ever be used.

For example, I have treated some alcoholics in recovery, who, although they have maintained abstinence for a good period of time—say 6 or 8 years—they have not been able to reach a state of "normal" and feel depressed or anxious. They will refuse to take medication, because they have learned that taking a mood-altering drug of any kind may trigger their disease, and they will "pick up" again. It's too extreme of a response.

And then, on the other side, some will immediately have recourse to medication. It is, for example, scary to learn about the numerous children who are on medications in order to help them "cope" with school. Again, it's too extreme.

There are several kinds of medications that help with mental/emotional symptoms. First there are the *anti-anxiety* drugs: those that aim to calm the nervous system. Often they are prescribed for agitation, phobias, performance anxiety, or panic attacks.

Anti-depressants are given to elevate one's mood: to regain interest in life/work; or to restore neurotransmitter balance to the body chemistry so the person will begin to enjoy life again. Anti-depressants are used for clinical depression, and recently for other symptoms. For example, they can be used for obsessive/compulsive disorder.

Next, *anti-psychotic* drugs are used for exaggerated or distorted perception of reality: when it is more a cognitive rather than an emotional disorder.

There are also other drugs for specific ailments: *narcotics* for pain; *antagonists* which are used to treat addictions; etc.

My point is not to give a review of medications, but to indicate that there are medications, which if used properly and under the supervision of a physician, can help attain a measure of serenity when interpersonal therapy does not work.

There is definitely a certain proportion of patients who can not be helped by the traditional methods of therapy. It doesn't make sense to run from therapist to therapist in the hope that you'll find the one who has the magic touch. It does make sense to turn to a psychopharmacologist, i.e. a doctor who is an expert in using medications for the "psyche"—for the soul.

"Bart" was a widower in his 60's, who had a series of losses, the most important of which was the loss of his wife. But there were other "bad luck" experiences—down-sizing, a son moving away, etc. He had been diagnosed as "grieving", i.e. going through a bereavement process. He had been going for bereavement therapy, which wasn't working. He called me up and I referred him first for a physical exam, with a recommendation for an evaluation for psychotropic drugs.

Once he was started on the correct regimen, he quickly returned to normal, without a long, searching review of "why" he was depressed.

Used properly, drugs can add to one's serenity, and you don't have to feel guilty about it.

Section VII—Letting Go

1. LETTING GO OF THE PAST LEADS TO SERENITY

Being a child of Italian immigrants, I zeroed in on a news article about Italian Americans. It was titled "Italian Americans on a quest for admission of wartime bias," and described how during WW II many Italians were labeled "enemy aliens" simply because they were of Italian descent.

Several celebrities joined a group who presented to Congress stories of how they were barred from work, or excluded from parts of society. For example, Joe DiMaggio's father was forbidden to go to Joe's restaurant in Fisherman's Wharf, and at the same time his other son, Dominic, was serving in the U.S. Navy.

"And so it goes." In the words of Kurt Vonnegut.

Japanese Americans were sequestered in camps during the same war. Blacks have an ignominious history of slavery; of being treated unfairly in our national wars. Women have been treated as chattel throughout history, and deprived of their rights in many ways. ACOA (adult children of alcoholics) were abused by alcoholic parents. Jews were persecuted in the name of religion, ethnic cleansing and state security.

"And so it goes."

And you know what? The trouble with claiming victimization is **that it is true!** In other words, as a statement

Vincent B. Cardarelli, Th.M., CADC

of historical fact, each one of these cultural and political evils can't be disproved—they are factual and true.

For the USA to deny that these things happened;
For Europe—esp. Nazi Germany—to deny the atrocities;
For men to deny that women were unjustly treated;
To deny that these things happened, or even worse, to seek to justify them is patently wrong.

It's only natural to blame, and if there is no one to blame, then we blame "God."

But for victims to remain victims by blaming the **past** for their **present** situation is to avoid responsibility.

Accepting responsibility for the present is not to exculpate, or forget, the past. We need to get along with one another **now**.

The Serenity Prayer says: God grant me the serenity to accept the things that I cannot change, the courage to change the things I can, and the wisdom to know the difference.

Your present agitation may have been caused by any of the following: a) the past infidelity of a spouse; b) the past injustice of a friend; c) the past atrocities of conflict or war; d) the sins or "dysfunction" of our parents; e) or whatever.

The way to serenity is—not to forget, God forbid—but to **forgive**…to let go of the animosity, the hurt, the desire for revenge or retaliation. I am not talking about something that happens here and now, or recently between two people or between groups.

When you hold on to blaming someone, you absolve yourself of doing anything about your misery. Fixing the blame, assigning fault puts you on a higher moral plane. And that feels good—**but** it doesn't change a thing, and it doesn't make you feel any better.

Iyanla Vanzant is an African American best-selling author of self-help books. She is a black former welfare mother who overcame rape, an abusive husband, poverty and teen-age pregnancies. Her message is "You have to do the work. As long as you can find one excuse...you will never have what you say you want."

Victor Frankl is a death camp survivor, a psychiatrist, and author of *Man's Search For Meaning*. He says that serenity requires that you "say yes to life in spite of...pain, guilt and death. Can life retain its potential meaning in spite of its tragic aspects?"

And when Peter asked Jesus how many times he should forgive his enemies..."up to seven times?" The Master answered: "...up to seventy times seven."

Lastly, Michael Palmer, in his novel *The Patient*, says "Holding on to resentment is like taking poison while waiting for the other guy to die."

Holding on to the 'tragic aspects' of the past in order to give meaning to the present only prolongs the suffering and prevents you from accepting the responsibility 'of doing the work.'

2. LETTING GO #2

A Crucial Step Toward Serenity

Learning to "let go" is a part of living; it's necessary to move on to the next phase of your life.

At a conference I once attended, a leaflet was distributed with the following text. The author is reputedly unknown, so I can't give the proper credit. However, read it slowly and meditatively. Another chapter will follow this one on the topic of 'letting go," which will outline what it is and how to practice it in everyday life.

Letting Go

To "let go" does not mean to stop caring, it means I can't do it for someone else.

To "let go" is not to cut myself off, it's the realization I can't control another.

To "let go" is not to enable, but to allow learning from natural sequences.

To "let go" is to admit powerlessness, which means the outcome is not in my hands.

To "let go" is not to try to change or blame another. It's to make the most of myself.

To "let go" is not to care for, but to care about.

To "let go" is not to fix, but to be supportive.
To "let go" is not to judge, but to allow another to be a human being.
To "let go" is not to be in the middle arranging all the outcomes, but to allow others to affect their own destinies.
To "let go" is not to be protective, it's to permit another to face reality.
To "let go" is not to deny, but to accept.
To "let go" is not to nag, scold or argue, but instead to search out my own shortcomings and correct them.
To "let go" is not to adjust everything to my desires but to take each day as it comes, and cherish myself in it.
To "let go" is not to regret the past, but to grow and live for the future.
To "let go" is to fear less and love more.

I'm sure you agree these are noble sentiments. But they are also action statements. Let's take a look at some situations that can often be resolved by letting go.

I am not suggesting that letting go is the only way to solve problems or conflict; only that sometimes letting go works best.

Other strategies are indeed also effective for handling the problems that follow, but unless one is able to "choose" the option of letting go, then such a person is locked into fruitless attempts at trying to control people and circumstances that often are essentially uncontrollable.

Unless one is able to let go, he is "stuck" in old behaviors, and thus trapped in repeating old arguments and conflicts.

When spouses have disagreements, if one is able at times to let go of his own point of view, or his own need to win a point, the disagreements evaporate.

When choices need to be made in families or between lovers, letting go can be a calm solution.

Vincent B. Cardarelli, Th.M., CADC

When your children face a "dangerous" experience, as parents, you are sometimes better off letting go of the need to control your child and letting him experience for himself.

When a friend or relative makes a mistake, letting go of redress is an eloquent sign of love. When you're hurt—at work, an action, a thoughtless or forgetful moment—letting go of the hurt repairs the relationship.

When you don't get your way, letting go is a way of coping with false pride.

When the past rises up in a kaleidoscope of flashbacks, letting go of the resentments allows you to keep talking, and to mend the relationship.

When you are tempted to 'blame' a loved one, letting go of that urge at "one-upmanship" shows maturity.

When your first love (high school or older) wants to break up, letting go works better than holding on.

When you need to discipline your children, letting go of the urge to punish allows you to think of other ways to get your point across.

When you are forced to move to a new home, letting go of the former frees you to enjoy the new.

When your friends move away, eventually you need to let go, not of memories, but of the pain of separation.

When you lose your job, letting go of the disappointment and anger frees you to attend to the task of finding and succeeding in the new one.

When a friend or relative dies, letting go is part of the process known as grief, and is the hardest part of bereavement.

When you get old, letting go lets you enjoy the present instead of living in the past.

In short, when I have to "move on," I am unable to do so until and unless I "let go."

Ah, yes. All through this chapter, you have been saying: But that's hard to do. And you're right! Movies, music and literature all attest to the poignant grief associated with changes, losses, breakups and death, and the pain involved in the "tragic" aspects of life. "Letting go" hurts, and so you don't let go voluntarily and happily. We usually kick and scream until there is no other choice.

The next chapter deals with the *how to* of letting go, and the part it plays in our struggle to find serenity.

3. LETTING GO #3

Letting go shows inner strength

There are so many self-help books that give you "how-to's—how to achieve inner peace, how to take charge of your life, how to communicate more effectively, how to tell your boss off, etc.

Each one of these methods tells you how to use a specific coping strategy which will help you to manage life and thus become a more mature, effective person.

"Letting go" is almost like a *non*-strategy. By not reacting, it allows you to cope with situations in which the other methods don't work.

Other strategies depend on a technique, a step-by-step plan to cope with conflict, stress, anxiety, resentments, etc. "Letting go" depends more on a conviction, or a feeling that although I am important and unique—and I am that—nevertheless I am not the only one who counts. Others are also important; their opinions and feelings are as important as mine.

"Letting go" is only possible when my image of myself is a good one, when I am secure in myself and I trust that I am OK. If everything doesn't always go my way, I'm still OK. I can let go of my opinion or whatever, and I'm still OK. And

TOWARD SERENITY

the world is still OK, too. I haven't really *lost* anything by letting go.

So the first trait that one needs to be able to let go, is to have enough self-esteem to stand on one's own two feet, and not be emotionally dependent on getting one's way.

Secondly, one needs to believe that ultimately "We are not in control." Life is often random; fate often determines more than we do. Life is what happens while we're making other plans.

Contrary to those who "EST" their way through life, or "who pull their own strings," or who follow "the American dream," or "who can be whatever they want"—more often than not, what happens to us is more a result of factors which we cannot control.

St. Paul said (loose translation): What I plan on doing, I end up not doing, and vice versa.

Another author put is this way: THE GREAT TRUTH is anything can happen. THE GREAT HALF-TRUTH is I can do anything I want to. THE GREAT LIE is I can be anyone I want to.

And so it is a valuable tool to be able to "chill out," to "go with the flow," to "let go." Not always, obviously. But there is a certain freedom in being able to let go, and still be happy. I peacefully solve my own problems. I avoid conflicts. And when other strategies don't work I still have one that allows me to rise above the fray.

When numerous efforts and ingenious plans have proved fruitless, and when all else fails, common sense and a practical philosophy of life calls for "letting go."

Maybe some of you will say that you are leery of that approach—that is sounds suspiciously like giving in, or giving up, which is the stuff of failure and being taken advantage of.

Not so. "Letting go" means an easy-going, non-aggressive secure acceptance of what is, and as a result experiencing a serenity, a peace, a oneness with a greater

Vincent B. Cardarelli, Th.M., CADC

force, a higher power, a God (if you will). That attitude is what is meant by the 12-Step phrase:
   Let go and Let God.

Section VIII—Spirituality and Faith

1. ON THE NEED FOR FAITH IN OUR QUEST FOR SERENITY

Many of you remember the Ballantine beer Three-Ring logo: Purity, Body and Flavor. They were three rings entwined in such a way that only a section of each was superimposed on the others. This resulted in an area that was shared by each.

An individual's health is somewhat like that: three parts—physical, emotional and cognitive—each distinct yet each connected in some way with the other two.

In order to have physical health, all parts of the body need to function well, otherwise a person is disabled. In order to have emotional health, one needs to experience all the feelings and behave in accord with them. In order to cognitive health, one needs to perceive the world outside objectively and organize the world and his relationship to it in a logical way. Good health, and thus, Serenity, depends on healthy "rings."

The third ring- cognitive health—must have a belief system or what we call "faith". What we believe gives meaning to our life. Cognitive health includes other components, like intellect and imagination, but it must also have a *belief system.*

Faith—or what we believe in—is the organizing principle in the third ring. Not only do we need to think

Vincent B. Cardarelli, Th.M., CADC

logically, and perceive with our senses what is out there, but we also have to be convinced that it all makes sense. Making sense of it is what faith provides.

An *atheist* is one who believes that there is no God, that there is no Superior Being. An *agnostic* is one who, when he looks outside, comes to the conclusion that he can't really prove either way the existence of a Superior Being. A *believer* is one who accepts the fact that there is a Higher Power.

Some believers will go to great lengths to explain *who* and *what* that Being is like: God, Allah, Jesus, etc. Others, like A.A., will be satisfied with a Higher Power. And still others will make a God of themselves.

When we believe only in ourselves, we make ourselves into God. It is called grandiosity, or pride. It's a great temptation, especially in modern days, to *believe* that you (the big Ego) can handle anything. "You can be all that you want", "you can do anything you want," "reach for the stars."

"Faith is not knowledge of what the mystery of the universe is, but the conviction that there IS a mystery, and that it is greater than us." Rabbi David Wolpe wrote that.

Rabbi Wolpe started out as a non-believer, and came to faith via his Jewish tradition, feeling that he could conquer his pride only by becoming a Rabbi.

On the other hand, I started out with a very structured and strict belief system, Catholicism. Eventually, I was ordained a priest. For me, at the time, the Catholic Faith gave meaning to my life and my belief allowed me to make sense of the world. I found serenity in the answers it provided.

But just as physical or emotional health can be jeopardized by crisis, so was my "faith-health" threatened. I just couldn't see how a Just and Merciful God could send down tragedy and bad luck to the good, and rewards and goodies to the bad. And much more than that too.

TOWARD SERENITY

So I retired from the clergy, thinking that I could go it alone. I learned, however, that not only do I have to be healthy physically and emotionally, but I also have to be healthy spiritually—or cognitively—or in the matter of faith. Simply put, I need to believe in something. I need to have faith.

So now, I find myself pretty much like an adolescent, exploring what beliefs I can adhere to in order to have cognitive health. My serenity depends on the fact that I have to believe in something. There was a time when I was ready to throw out the baby with the bath water, so to speak. Now I "own" my faith. It has been forged by years of questioning and finding my own answers.

The next chapter focuses on "owned faith" which is pertinent here.

The A.A. program starts several of its 12 Steps with the words: "came to believe..." The wisdom of the A.A. program, as well as in all "self-help" programs is that each person who succeeds, does so by giving up the urge to control, to go it alone, to be prideful. Each person "comes to believe" that there is a power greater than himself out there to whom he needs to submit his will (see "The Thirteenth Step").

In order to heal a broken spirit, one needs to "surrender" without knowing all about who or what He (It) is. "Faith is not knowledge of what the mystery of the universe is."

Faith is "the conviction that there *IS* a mystery, and that it is greater than us." And really, isn't that what we are doing when we reach out to someone and ask for help? We are saying that we can't do it alone. That is the beginning of faith.

Amazingly, Serenity comes as a result. Whether it is the road that Rabbi Wolpe took,—from disbelief to the Rabbinate—, or whether it is the road that I took—from detailed belief to doubt to a more personal belief—or whether it is the road that you may take—whichever...As

Vincent B. Cardarelli, Th.M., CADC

long as you arrive at a belief that includes some meaning greater than yourself, you will have serenity.

2. 'OWNED FAITH' GIVES ANSWERS TO LIFE'S QUESTIONS

In Dymmoch's novel "Incendiary Designs," Caleb, the main character, attends the funeral of a friend, Manny. During the ride to the cemetery, Caleb remembers his tour of duty in the Marines.
The author writes the following:

> Caleb's belief in God had been formed in Vietnam. The childhood (faith) inherited from his parents, to which he'd paid lip service in his youth, had been blown away by the first hostile fire, when an enemy round tore a life-ending hole in the chest of his comrade.
> But a journalist he'd (met in a foxhole) had given him a kind of palliative substitute for his lost naïveté'.
> "If God follows His own rules," the writer had said, "He is as powerless to stop this war as we are."
> "How can you say that?" asked Caleb.
> "God gave us free will. You're not really free if you're not free to f— up. And He gave us history and Machiavelli to learn from. You're not free if you're not allowed to forget, or to ignore the lesson in the first place. So don't blame God. *We* did this ourselves."

Vincent B. Cardarelli, Th.M., CADC

>Caleb thought of that (conversation) whenever something occurred that seemed senseless or ironically tragic.
>*Free will.*
>Free will and accident could account for all the misery laid at the feet of God. In the beginning, God had created accident. It was an oversight that it wasn't mentioned in Genesis, but the Scripture writers probably hadn't been as thoughtful or as imperiled as Caleb's journalist. And God was stuck with (what was not written.)
>However, the insight made God irrelevant for Caleb, but it also made Caleb stop blaming God for things, let him stop hating Him.

In the course of his life experiences, Caleb had developed what one inspirational writer calls "owned faith".

D. Westerhoff, a theologian, lists four stages of faith; "faith" being the doctrines that people profess in their religious communities. The first kind of faith is called: *experienced faith.* This is the early stage, when young children do and say what their parents have taught them. They *experience* what is around them and in a sense, follow the leader.

It is certainly valid, and works for them in the early ages. Stories are told, which make sense to the children at their age; rituals and scriptures are part of their experience and help them to make sense of the world.

The next stage is *affiliative faith.* Usually around the ages 6-12, the growing child takes a more active part in the religious practices (formal or just in the home.) He now affiliates with a community: parish, synagogue or other religious group. He is not just "going along," but begins to be indoctrinated in the beliefs and morals of his group. He also begins to identify with it, and in fact finds some of his own identity in the affiliation.

TOWARD SERENITY

During this time, the adolescent can be quite dedicated to the faith, and even find models and heroes from the religious group to which he adheres.

This is the stage when Confirmation, and Bar-Mitzvahs take place, and such rituals are perfectly acceptable to the adolescent, and they are meaningful within the context of the stage that he finds himself.

The next stage is *searching faith.* This is the stage that gives gray hairs to parents and to religious leaders. The young adult, from around 16-to maturity, now begins to question the doctrines. He wants to test what he has learned and heard, and see if it fits his own experience. It is a stage of moral and spiritual development.

Rather than being threatened by this uncertain period, parents and guardians of the "Faith" need to encourage the search, and trust that at the end of the tunnel, the seeker of truth will come up with his **own** faith.

The fourth stage is exactly that: *owned faith.* This is the kind of faith attained by Caleb in the example above. It is the filtered down and digested version of the experienced and affiliated faith of youth, which will now be of service to him in his adult life.

So many people are "turned off" by the faith of their childhood. Maybe it is not excusable, but it is understandable, since the things they learned as children do not have the answers to the questions and experiences of adulthood.

It is essential, then, to examine and evaluate what was handed down to us, and search sincerely for a faith that fits our experiences. It doesn't mean that you simply throw out the faith of our fathers; in fact, it may mean that you actually come back to it. But it may also mean that you will be forced to tailor it to your own life experiences. And as a result your version of "faith" may be different from others.

The senseless and tragic events—the accidental and unintended horrors that are the result of the free will of sick

Vincent B. Cardarelli, Th.M., CADC

or evil people—cannot be blamed on God. That is a conclusion of youthful, unexamined faith.

So in the words of the journalist in the story above: "Don't blame God. We did it ourselves."

3. FALSE PRIDE

There seems to be an innate tendency toward pride. It is quite common for a person to think of himself as better than others. The average person does not see himself as being "average.'

There exists a pervasive self-serving bias in the way we perceive ourselves as compared to others, and in the way we interpret events that happen to us.

Try this experiment: Ask your friends to complete this sentence: "My guess is that a certain percent of my friends and co-workers are more...than I am." Then tell them to fill in the space with a positive character trait, such as "sympathetic," "responsible" or "considerate." Finally, ask them to assess what the percentage is of friends and/or co-workers that fits the description. Usually the percent is a modest one.

Another way in which people see themselves as being better than average is in games of skill or chance. At cards, for example, when one wins he attributes it to skill, and when he loses, there is always an external reason—lousy cards, luck, etc.

When we are given compliments for our good behavior, we take credit for it; but when we are accused of nasty or inconsiderate behavior, we quickly find scape-goats for it. "Sure I was angry, but that was because everything was going wrong."

Therapists take credit for successful outcomes with their patients, but blame failure on the person being helped.

An article in *Psychology Today* reported a number of experiments which showed that almost everyone ranging from 12 years old to adults perceived of himself as somehow superior.

The other side of the coin is that most of us see our friends, neighbors and classmates as a sorry lot. They are morally weaker: *Guess what Betty did...*more intolerant: *I couldn't believe it when John said...*and less intelligent: *Saying what she said really takes the cake...*

This self-serving bias is often personally useful. It may even be a trait that has been bred into us through natural selection. Thinking positively about myself and about my talents may give me the extra push I need to have the self-confidence leading to success.

Self-serving bias, called human pride, is not usually a fatal attraction. However, all forms of literature, beginning with the Bible where pride led to the expulsion from Eden, down to modern day novels, are filled with examples of excessive pride that leads to deception and tragedy.

Nations are drawn into international conflict when each side believes that it is morally superior to the other, and therefore justified in acts of war toward the enemy.

On the other hand, politicians are well-served by this self-deception, especially when they compare themselves to other candidates in the campaign.

It is a different story when pride (superiority) shows itself in a relationship. Conflict occurs similar to warring nations. Each partner sees himself or herself as morally superior—better than average—to the other. Each sees his opinion and judgment as true and honest; and each sees the other as blameworthy or less intelligent.

But the stumbling block to serenity is that becoming aware of my own tendency to see myself as "better" is like "trying to see my own eyeball." It is hard to see myself as I really am.

The cure for this false pride, this human trait, is humility. Humility is not self-flagellation, nor is it self-contempt, nor false modesty. It doesn't mean that one has to belittle his own qualities so as not to insult or hurt others. It does not mean that a handsome person has to believe or act as if he is ugly.

True humility is more like self-forgetfulness. You can rejoice in your own truth and accomplishments, while at the same time rejoice in the truth and accomplishments of your friend or acquaintance. True humility is an honest self-appraisal, warts and all, of yourself and of others.

C.S. Lewis wrote: "There is no fault which we are more unconscious of in ourselves...(than human pride). If anyone would like to acquire humility, I can, I think, tell him the first step. The first step is to realize that one is proud."

That is pretty big step on the way to serenity.

4. THE SPIRITUALITY OF IMPERFECTION

In the story of the Garden of Eden, the serpent tempted Adam and Eve with the promise that "they would be like God" if they "ate of the forbidden fruit." In their misguided attempt to "know all" and be like God, they fell, i.e. they became aware of their own imperfections.

Is this a story about sin, or a primitive myth that explains our essential imperfection?

Many religions teach their congregations to "seek perfection" as the spiritual goal. That was the message I got growing up: namely, that I had to strive to be sinless and pure. And if I was not, then I couldn't go to Communion (not a member of the elect), and I was in jeopardy of losing heaven. And try as I might I simply never got there.

Even though confession and forgiveness were built into the belief system, it was not considered "spiritual" to be imperfect.

Therapy is like that too, since it promises that you can "fulfill your potential," or that every problem can be solved. Often therapists hold out a goal that is unattainable. "Be all that you can be..." "Don't accept the status quo; you can change what makes you unhappy."

But authors *Ernest Kurtz* and *Katherine Ketcham*, in their book *The Spirituality of Imperfection,* maintain that perfection is an impossible goal. They propose a spirituality that is based on the fact that we are essentially imperfect, and will remain that way.

The point of the book is that you'll be less stressed if you accept the limitations that your own imperfections place on you. The spirituality of imperfection is based on what in the human being is irrevocable and immutable: namely, the basic and inherent flaws of being human. Errors are part of the game—something like baseball, where if you are successful one third of the time, you're considered a star. Baseball also keeps a record of errors and losses; it's part of the game. You're expected not to be perfect all the time.

Bill Wilson, the founder of AA, never did get religion, but he did say: "We must find some *spiritual basis* for living, else we die." That saying is nothing new in the history of various religions, but it is different from the fundamentalist view of religion, which says that perfection is the ideal. If you die in the state of sin, they teach, you cannot enter the pearly gates.

Many people are turned off by organized religion because it claims to be *right;* it claims to have the inspired truth from God. And so *spirituality* by definition means perfection. The spirituality of imperfection, on the other hand, makes no claim to be right. Imperfection is the norm, and by coming to terms with errors and shortcomings, you can find peace and serenity.

You need to ACCEPT that you are unable to control every aspect of your life, and that in some ways you will fall short of your own expectations.

One of the benefits of this kind of approach is that you'll be less defensive. So when your spouse or your parent points out something about you that irritates them or hurts them, you won't have to fight back or give lame excuses about your substandard behavior.

Vincent B. Cardarelli, Th.M., CADC

Kurtz/Ketcham quote a story from the Far East in their book to illustrate *the spirituality of imperfection:*

> The great master Mat-su, as a youth, was a fanatic about sitting in meditation for many hours at a time. One day, his patriarch's disciple Huai-jang asked him what on earth he hoped to attain by this compulsive cross-legged sitting.
> "Buddhahood," said Mat-su.
> Thereupon Huai-jang sat down, took a brick, and started to polish it assiduously. Mat-su looked at him, perplexed, and asked what he was doing.
> "Oh," said Huai-jang, "I am making a mirror out of my brick."
> "You can polish it till doomsday," scoffed Mat-su, "you'll never make a mirror out of a brick!"
> "Aha!" smiled Huai-jang. "Maybe you are beginning to understand that you can sit until doomsday, it won't make you into a Buddha."

As hard as it is to accept my own imperfections, it is even harder to accept the imperfection of others. It's a great temptation to tell others what they ought to do. Remember the musical, *Man of La Mancha?* The relatives of Don Quixote sang: "I'm only thinking of you..." That was the reason they gave to justify their attempts at changing him. But the real reason was that they themselves wouldn't be embarrassed by his tilting at windmills. When you try to correct or control loved ones, so they'll become better persons, you play God. To accept imperfection as the norm, both for oneself as well as for others, is to avoid playing God.

The spirituality of imperfection does not say: "I'm OK, You're OK;" instead it says "I'm not OK; you're not OK, *BUT that's OK.*" It's not that you seek imperfection; it's that you learn to live with it and in spite of it.

5. AH! SWEET MYSTERY OF LIFE

Let's Not Explain It Away

Nelson Eddy sang to Jeanette MacDonald in his rich baritone: "Ah! Sweet mystery of life at last I've found you." After searching for love, he found in Jeanette the quality that had been missing until then.

We are in a highly scientific and technological age where mostly everything can be explained, or "if you can imagine it, then it can be done."

I have a certain nostalgia for the days of my childhood, when there was a mysterious quality about events and experiences that could not be fully explained and even less understood.

The "mysterious" has all but gone out of modern life. We seem compelled to make our lives anthropocentric, that is, interpreting reality exclusively in terms of human values and experiences, all of which can be understood and explained.

The "mysterious" is, according to the dictionary, that which simultaneously arouses and eludes the desire to know, comprehend or explain. Mysterious, or mystery, is usually applied to religious things, phenomena which have an untouchable reality but nevertheless have meaning for the believer. The mysterious generates our sense of wonder.

However, like the mystery play of old, it seems that the mystical has been relegated to the past.

When we kids entered a church, our behavior was determined by the mysterious. We spoke, if at all, in hushed voices. We sang and prayed lustily, but as we knelt in the presence of the mysterious, there was a reverence, enhanced by incense and votive candles, toward what was not fully understood, but nonetheless real and powerful.

Although we knew that the Virgin Mary was not divine, we spoke of her with reverence, and this we learned was to be extended to all women and especially to our mothers. It made sense. Maybe some men condescended to women, but the ideal was there and no one questioned it.

Something has been lost in our effort to make Mary merely human, and women more like men. Maybe with more mystery, we'd have more respect for women.

An article in the magazine JANE is entitled "I sold my eggs..." It sounded modern, egalitarian, and even altruistic. But the "sweet mystery" of life and of the awesome fact of its transmission is missing from the article. It is scientific, prodigious and amazing, but it is neither mysterious nor reverent.

"A better life through chemicals" fuels a large part of our economy. Will Viagra add "sweet mystery" to love between spouses, or will it provide only better technology?

No matter what ailment, no matter what feeling we want to enhance or prevent, no matter how imperfectly the brain performs, there is a drug, legal or illegal, that promises to make it better.

Should we do away with the effort to make things better? No. But it seems that we are losing the mysterious quality of our lives—that "God is watching us from a distance." In our attempt to live a better life, there are some things beyond our ken, and we need to approach them with awe and reverence.

The counselor's office has supplanted the confessional. The stethoscope has replaced the prayer shawl. Freedom from sickness is more important than freedom from sin. Money, power and fame are the present day Trinity.

Is this all bad? Certainly not.

Sure, explaining everything by faith can be carried too far. For example, when a tragedy occurs, like a train wreck that kills hundreds of people, or an illness that strikes down a young child—or even 9/11—some will say "It's God's will," or "It was meant to be." I'd call that "blind faith," but not "mysterious."

So it takes a sense of awe, a sense of humility to be able to acknowledge that there is something greater than me out there, and try as I might, my finite mind will not be able fully to comprehend that greater power.

Maybe there is not this kind of God, or that kind of God, but the mysterious keeps man's pride within bounds, and keeps us from playing God.

The mysterious allows us to have serenity when faced with things we can't entirely figure out for ourselves.

6. DISCERNMENT

Following the crowd won't give serenity

The quest for serenity is ongoing. Human nature being what it is, we tend to lose it from time to time, especially when confronted with conflict or having to make moral choices. It's especially true when the choice you have to make goes against the prevailing opinion, or the pressure of the crowd.

Do you remember the day that the voluminous Kenneth Starr report on President Clinton was released to the public, complete with videos, etc? "It's all out there now for each person to make up his own mind," said the pundits. Oh, Yeah? Well, just how do we make up our own mind?

Just think for a minute about the amount of information that comes at us from the TV or the Internet. Newspapers bombard us with both information and conclusions. How to select what to listen to, not to mention what to believe?

How do children, and the adults who guide them, sort through the barrage and retrieve what is important and discard what is not?

It is then that the power of "discernment" helps out. To "discern" is to be able to discriminate, to perceive the inherent differences, to show insight and judgment. Discernment is the keenness or special ability to be perceptive and see beyond the obvious. One is able to discern the truth, or the essence behind the obvious.

Unless we can do it for ourselves, we are in danger of being led around by he nose. There are plenty of examples of that in history where the masses have followed some ideologue. If you're a Republican, you vote the party line; if you're a Democrat, same thing. If you're an Independent, you talk a good game, but what do you do on Election Day? Stay home? If you're a Palestinian, are you free to see some truth in an Israeli position? And vice-versa.

Recently, I watched a program that followed a political speech. Two senators sat side by side in front of a TV camera. Each was asked the same question and one gave one answer, and the other gave exactly the opposite. Neither could find any area of agreement. Who's right? How do you decide for yourself—or do you?

That is exactly the point, you see. For your own serenity, you need to ask: Can I decide for myself? Can I withhold judgment? Can I pick and choose from both sides and come up with my own compromise?

Conflicts exist in every life, especially in the lives of adolescents who are in the process of 'becoming" individuals. How to withstand "peer pressure?"

The virtue of discernment not only empowers you to make judgments, it also gives you peace and satisfaction within, no matter what the turmoil is outside.

Well, now, you can't go around like a computer and be "discerning" all the time. Sometimes you go with the flow and just have fun. The enjoyment is being part of a crowd or a group. Like when I went with my daughter and her friends to a Maze, carved out of a corn field. The fun was getting lost as well as finding our way.

But sometimes, especially when you're overwhelmed with input (stressors) from the outside, you need to back off and be discriminating, to be able to pick and choose, and not to follow the crowd. Instead, you "follow your own bliss."

Vincent B. Cardarelli, Th.M., CADC

Following the crowd is not a prescription for serenity, or for spirituality. The word "discernment" is often used in spiritual discourse, referring to the gift that God gives to be able to recognize His Will. But I think it has great application also for seekers of serenity; it helps us see through the non-essentials and get to the heart of the matter.

7. SIC TRANSIT GLORIA MUNDI

A Reminder That All the Glories of the World
Are Fleeting

After the coronation of a newly elected Pope, he is carried in the Sede Gestatoria (the ceremonial throne) in a procession from the Sistine Chapel through St. Peter's Square and down the aisle of St. Peter's Basilica to preside at his first function as the leader of the Catholic Church. Walking in front of the Pope's chair, there is an attendant who carries a plate on which burn into ashes some palms, at the same time repeatedly intoning *"sic transit Gloria mundi,"* which means "Thus passeth the glory of the world."

It is a reminder to the Pope that everything, especially the power and glory associated with such a high position as the Papacy, is transitory, turning into ashes. Now you have it and now you don't.

Well, this was certainly brought home to me during the past couple of years, during which all the temporal goods and titles that I have amassed seem less important. My health, which I have been blessed with and have always taken for granted, seems more tenuous.

In the space of one year four of my uncles, all my mother's brothers, died. The last one, Pat, died during the

Vincent B. Cardarelli, Th.M., CADC

Christmas holidays. Certainly a reminder to me of the passing nature of all that I possess.

Uncle Pat was more like my big brother. Since he was only a few years older than I, we grew up together until he went off into the service of WWII. I had looked on him as my model, and the person after whom I tried to pattern myself. I never quite succeeded, and now that he is gone, I am sorry that I never told him about how important he was to me.

He was a man who was larger than life. He could have, if he had a voice, sung Frank Sinatra's *I Did It My Way,* and it would have reflected how he lived.

But even for him, *sic transit...*

This experience, the loss of immediate family, has made me pause and think: what about me? What "glories" have I held on to and considered important?

We begin a new millennium. The daily papers and the magazines predict astounding discoveries and successes in telecommunications and medicine. We become puffed up with our own importance, and with our control over our lives and destinies.

"You can be anything you want to." We plan for the future with unbounded confidence and bravado.

We are like the Pope riding in his Sede Gestatoria, anticipating great things ahead.

We need to be reminded that all the glory of the world, and all the power amassed, and all that we have accumulated, and all the security we have stashed in IRA's or whatever...vanishes into ashes sooner than we think. Sic transit...

Attending yet another wake recently, I heard clergy, family and friends trying to make sense of what had happened to a life unfulfilled. I heard numerous mourners resolving to finish what they had intended to do and never got done; or visit the places they always wanted to see, etc.

There's nothing like a tragedy, or a death, or a severe illness to put things into perspective. We seem to be willing to view the bigger picture when confronted with traumatic events.

But when we are riding the crest of success, health, wealth, power and glory, we get caught up in the triumphant feelings and tend to ignore that *this too shall pass.*

Our serenity does not depend on the external and material things. It is tempting to be so caught up in our riches and pleasures, that we think we have the world by the tail. Serenity depends on internal values and attitudes, a way of life that enjoys but does not depend on possession, power and prestige.

Don't get me wrong: I am not advocating that the rich give away all their possessions to the poor, like St. Francis of Assisi. Nor am I saying that the poor should be grateful for their lot in life, because they are really the lucky ones, and are a shoo-in for serenity.

The point to be made is that the attraction and gratification of power and glory are strong temptations to lure a person away from what really produces lasting happiness. If we need more proof of that, all we have to do is look at the fact that even though we have more of everything in the 21st century—more years to live, more money to spend, more gadgets to make life easier, in short *more*—even so, larger numbers of men, women and children are taking feel-good drugs, and using substitute ways of alleviating pain. It makes you stop and think.

Sic transit Gloria mundi.

8. FORGIVENESS

Seeking and Granting Forgiveness as A Way Toward Serenity

The Rev. Jerry Falwell was on the Geraldo show talking about forgiveness of President Clinton. What he defined as forgiveness sounded more like retribution and righteousness.

Forgiveness is of the essence of mental as well as spiritual health. It is the Cinderella virtue of serenity. It is skirted around when talking about peace between individuals and nations. It's the last thing one wants to face and deal with. Why? Because it is the last vestige of accepting responsibility for your own happiness.

Forgiveness is essential for mental and emotional health. As an example, try this out: Make a list of the resentments that you harbor—those things you just can't forget about, much less forgive. Against your spouse, your errant children, your boss, the company that demoted you, etc.

Holding on to those resentments, a stockpiling of past angers, upsets the balance of your serenity. They raise your blood pressure, they cause you to be vulgar, and to generate evil thoughts to desire revenge. Most of all, they cause you to be alienated from those who you are close to. There are plenty of examples—husband and wife, neighbor and neighbor, Falwell and Clinton, Israel and Palestine.

Imagine what you would feel like if you were FREE of those resentments. Definitely a lot happier.

Forgiveness is also essential for spiritual health. Christianity, and all religions, are based on the foundation of forgiveness. "Revenge is mine, saith the Lord." "I say unto you, forgive your enemies, do good to those that hate you."

In the past, I've been terminated from a job, betrayed by a friend and unfairly accused as a professional. What do you think would happen to my serenity if I held on to their injustices? (Well, I have to confess that I did hold on for a long time.)`

Forgiveness means to free yourself of the burden of hurt and injustice caused by the offender. It is to rid your heart of the animosity and resentments lodged there. It doesn't mean to excuse them, or to "plea bargain" away any need for resolution. Pope John Paul gave an example of this when he forgave Sirhan Sirhan, his would-be assassin.

It means to "grant pardon" without harboring resentment. Hard to do—remember the outrage when President Ford pardoned Nixon? It means to pass over a transgression or fault without demanding punishment or redress. Like the amnesty granted to the Vietnam draft resisters.

It does NOT mean eliminating restitution. It is an obligation of the offending party to "make amends," to repair the grievance or injustice that was committed. If someone steals from me, I can forgive him. That takes care of my serenity. But he still needs to "give back" what was taken. That will take care of his—the thief's spiritual problem. I need to forgive; he needs to seek forgiveness.

If I hurt someone and seek forgiveness, I need to make it right. If I forgive someone, I can grant it in my heart, but I can't excuse what was done. That is the offender's job.

Granting pardon has the added quality of not seeking restitution. Getting back or retaliating doesn't give me serenity, but forgiveness does. Not to forgive, and holding on to resentment and hurt, makes *me* hateful and bitter. "Harboring resentment is like taking poison while waiting for the other person to die." (Michael Palmer in *The Patient*).

To forgive is to "Let Go and Let God," that is, letting a higher power be the judge and the one who will ultimately restore the balance, or solve the problem. For a believer, it means turning it over to God. For a non-believer, it means "working it through," much like a grief process. For both, forgiveness is an expression of spirituality.

There is a similarity between good religion and good therapy. Both seek to bring together warring partners or enemies. Both seek resolution of conflict. The proverb says "There is no resolution without confrontation." That's not one hundred percent true: a conflict can be resolved by forgiveness.

There is no solution for racism, for bigotry, for alienation between parent and children (or between nations) without forgiveness. The U.S. went through a ceremony of forgiveness with Japan. What would have happened if both demanded retribution? We'd still be at war, or maybe just a "cold war."

Forgiveness is not wishy-washy. It is not a weakling's way of solving a problem. Mental health calls it a "coping strategy" and religion calls it a "gathering in communion." Those who have attained spirituality will pick themselves up and go on in spite of the losses and tragedies that befall them along the way.

Oh, yes! It is easy to sit in judgment of others, demanding in our righteousness that "justice be done." Such a person is indeed *morally right*, but can hardly be called charitable or healthy. Kahlil Gibran says: "He who wears his morality but as his best garment were better naked."

To receive forgiveness or to give forgiveness produces a sense of freedom and serenity.

9. CUTTING CORNERS ON HONESTY

They say there are three kinds of lies: lies, white lies, and statistics. There is another kind of lie that technically is not a lie, nor a white lie. But it is a damn thing, nonetheless.

It's called the "cutting corners" kind of lie and it's so easy to succumb to that temptation and still call it "honest". In fact, it's so easy that it happens everywhere: at work, in relationships, in business and in advertisements.

It happens at work. Employees call in sick, when they are not. Employers promise benefits which they don't deliver. Both rationalize: "It's not exactly a lie": the employee says that he is entitled to the sick days; and the employer says that in the future things will change, and for now he is honest.

As a result, both labor and management have a relationship of distrust, whereby each expects the other to be telling what is called a "half-truth." Each feels justified in cutting corners on honesty.

It happens in relationships. A mother may protect her children from the wrath of their father by relating only part of what really happened. A husband may color his "going-out-of-town-on-business" trip to avoid his wife's suspicions. Children may tell only part of the truth of what happened in school, or whether they did their homework, or which friends will be at a party.

Vincent B. Cardarelli, Th.M., CADC

It happens in business. Contracts, sub-par materials, padding the bill. You can come up with your own examples of this one. My own example is that I just got notice that the "principals" of my IRA have engaged in misconduct and as a result I have no assurance that I will be receiving any of my savings.

It happens in advertisements. Cars, appliances, insurance coverage. You just know that those advertisements that promise that "we will absolutely not be undersold," are enticements only. "*Caveat emptor*"—Let the buyer beware.

We rationalize and justify this kind of interaction all the time. As long as my intention is good, or as long as "everybody knows" that "everybody does it," then I can bend the truth for whatever purpose I may have. The end justifies the means.

It's cutting corners; it's an easy way out It's avoidance, and it's cutting the corners on honesty.

Let me say that I am not a proponent of the commandment that you have to tell the truth, the whole truth, and nothing but the truth every time. You must do that when you are under oath.

And generally speaking, we should be honest. To be honest means that what is inside (your mind and heart) is the same as what is outside (your words and behavior). But there are times when prudence is the better part of valor, and what you know to be the truth (and nothing but), is better left unsaid.

To tell your boss what you really think; to tell your spouse what her dress really looks like—well, you may do better with a euphemism. I guess you can call that "cutting corners" too.

But when someone tells a half-truth, or a distortion of the truth, and maintains that it is "honest" is a whole different thing. That is what I mean by "cutting corners" on honesty. It is self-serving. It is worse even than telling an outright lie, because it erodes trust between two parties who have come together with the belief that each will be open and honest.

How can we live worry-free (serenely) in a society that is not based on an honest interchange of ideas, or of promises or commerce? How can we teach our children to behave in a moral and just manner, when we cut corners on honesty?

These are important questions we have to ask and *answer for ourselves.* In the midst of this pervasive dishonesty, we can easily become cynical and distrustful, and thus our serenity is in jeopardy.

In finding answers for ourselves, I think it's helpful to keep two conditions in mind. The first is that we ourselves avoid trickery. For example, in a recent article, columnist David Ignatius wrote: "Cops and FBI agents use deceptive tactics...in their effort to obtain the higher truth of a confession." Does a noble end justify unethical means to get there? Is it OK to trick someone into accepting a half-truth?

The second condition is to ask whether or not **in this situation** you have an *obligation* to tell the truth or to act honestly. For example, when you are transacting some business, or talking with a loved one, then cutting corners on honesty is just plain lying—not just a means to an end, but an end in itself. As such, it is wrong.

10. "CARPE DIEM" PHILOSOPHY REDUCES ANXIETY

You remember the movie *Dead Poets' Society* in which Robin Williams plays the lead role. He was a teacher in a prestigious school, and his theme was "carpe diem", which means literally "seize the day." Williams' character taught the philosophy that one should start the day with determination and verve, and thus he will accomplish a lot in life.

Implied in the *carpe diem* philosophy is the need to get started. Postponing and being undisciplined is contrary to the notion.

It's not so difficult to have a supervisor tell you what to do and when to do it. The concept of a 9 to 5 job, with your job specs listed doesn't require much internal discipline. But to be a self-starter, and to attend to the task until it is completed needs a motivation that comes from within. *Carpe diem* means that I don't need a parent nor a policeman nor a supervisor to get started and to stay on task to the finish.

The examples are legion. A home-owner who does not "pick-up" and leaves things around with the intention of getting to it. A student who waits until the last minute to do homework or a paper. One who is overweight and postpones starting a weight-loss regimen. One who starts with a bang, and loses steam leaving a number of tasks unfinished. As I said, there are lots of examples.

There are the perfectionists, who let it go until they have the time to do it right. Or they may leave it till the last minute, while keeping the task at the periphery of awareness. You can imagine the build-up of anxiety that occurs underneath the surface. Such anxiety is a threat to serenity.

There are the easy-going, creative types, who just don't like to be told what to do, and as a result things stack up either on the desk or the floor.

There are the "essentialists" who can't be bothered by detail; so they start something and never get it done, often leaving it to others to clean up behind them.

There are those who are detail-oriented; the ones who are getting ready to keep an appointment, but on the way, they straighten out the living room, or make a phone call, or wash the dishes in the sink before they get going. And so they are late, and get anxious that someone will be mad at them.

Maybe it's personality (what you were born with), or maybe it is style (what you acquired growing up), but either way what suffers is satisfaction—the sense of a job completed. It may not be a job *well-done*, but at least it is a job *done*.

You can't equate satisfaction with serenity, but lack of satisfaction does contribute to lack of serenity.

So the bottom line is *carpe diem*—get started. Take one thing at a time, look at it and get started. Don't let your attention get distracted by a "red herring" which crosses your path while you are on the way to something important.

After you have started it, get it finished. So what if it isn't perfect; most of our life is spent on enjoying what we could not have to the fullest anyway. Although we are told to "enjoy life to the fullest," most of what we experience is essentially imperfect.

Vincent B. Cardarelli, Th.M., CADC

Think about it. Whether it is a vacation, or a car, or the friends your children select, or your spouse, whatever it is, usually falls short of perfection.

I remember once that I worked for a harsh supervisor, who consistently sent back what I had written for revision. It wasn't good enough. So I soon learned to keep writing an imperfect document and sending it to her for correction, until she ended up writing it herself.

Then you have those who "talk the talk." That is, they keep talking about what they have to do, and analyze an issue continually, thus avoiding getting started. One needs the internal discipline to "walk the walk." In the addictions program, this means to stop drinking, or to stop smoking. To stop! Not to talk about it but to "do" it.

The ability to "Just Do It" (a la Nancy Reagan) is called internal discipline. Internal discipline means that you have inside of you the strength to follow through on what you decide you want to do. If it was not inculcated as a child, internal discipline is difficult to acquire as an adult. For some, that is not easy. It requires making a schedule and then sticking to it.

The slogan "One Day At A Time" reminds people in the "program" that the only way to achieve sobriety and serenity is to do it now, and not look into the future.

What works for me is *carpe* collar—that is grab myself by the back of the neck or by the collar, and in a sense force myself to get started or to stay on task. In other words, internal discipline.

But as I look up from my word processor, I see the dining room table littered with "work in progress," laundry that has not been folded and put away, dishes in the sink, unfinished chapters in my book sitting on my desk — aw, jeez, I'm getting anxious and I better interrupt myself here and finish this at a later date.

Section IX—The Thirteenth Step

1. THE THIRTEENTH STEP:

Serenity through surrender of the Ego

We've come to the final section of this book. It contains only one chapter entitled *The Thirteenth Step.* Many of the preceding chapters are inspired by the program known as "The 12 Step Program" and The Serenity Prayer. The spirit and philosophy of the steps are reflected throughout.

But there is more to serenity than the 12 steps. I've taken the liberty to compose a "13th" Step. By its composition and presentation here, I am attempting to summarize all the chapters in *Toward Serenity.* Obviously, there is no short cut to serenity or happiness; but neither is it possible to remember all the strategies and coping mechanisms that people like me throw at you. So I formulated the 13th Step in the hope that it could be like a *mantra* of this book.

It goes like this: *"I came to believe that my search for serenity depends upon a constant vigilance against false pride, a constant effort toward humility, and a submission of my will to a power greater than myself."* In short, the 13th Step says that serenity is acquired through surrender of the Ego. Let's break it down and explain it in detail.

Vincent B. Cardarelli, Th.M., CADC

Came to believe... After scrambling to find my own answers to the mysteries of life, and to "be anything I want to be, and do anything I want to do," I have finally come to the realization—the belief—that I am not totally in charge. I can't do it "My Way." Through bitter experience, I have come to accept certain truths which I can't prove and in fact, don't need to prove. I now believe...and my **belief** provides the answers that I couldn't find on my own.

My search for serenity... One of the truths I have learned is that serenity does not come in a package, nor is it a particular type of therapy which will work magic in me. I have learned that I need to keep on searching and struggling. It is a journey, and taking time to smell the flowers along the way will produce more peace and happiness than "arriving" at some promised land. Serenity is not getting what I want. The **search** is more important than the result **Depends upon a constant vigilance against false pride...**Another truth I have learned is "progress not perfection" is all I can realistically hope for. I need to be on guard against my own grandiosity, my own temptation to play God. That temptation sneaks up every-where: In my car, I think I am the King of the Road; In my home, I demand "respect:" In a group, I need to be recognized; Secretly, I think I am better than others.

My *ego*, my pride, puts constant pressure on me to be better; it tempts me to be haughty, vain, and pompous. I need to be "right" in arguments or in discussions with my family and spouse.

And so, as an antidote, I need to be vigilant—constantly - against this false pride, against my inflated ego. Such pride destroys serenity.

Depends upon a constant effort to be humble...I have also learned that I need to balance out my haughty self-importance and vanity with an equal amount of humility. It is true that I am a Child of God: that I am unique, one of a kind, and deserve all that the Constitution says that I have a right to. But it is also true that I am one of a crowd, and no better than anyone else. No one is better than me; but neither do I stand above others.

Humility does not mean "humiliation:" it means "truth." Sometimes it is difficult to face the truth about myself, and the truth is that I can't take myself too seriously. The effort to be humble results, paradoxically, in serenity.

We need to guard against false pride, and at the same time to seek humility...by that kind of vigilance, we will keep ourselves from self-deception, and from the temptation to play God. Paradoxically, it is when I am humble that I have the true strength of self-esteem.

Submission of my will to a power great than myself...Maybe I can't (or won't) accept a Personal God as my higher power, and maybe I can't go to a church or synagogue and submit my will to another man who speaks "in the name of God." Maybe I can't get religion to "save" me from my wrongs. But that is not the meaning of this phrase in the 13th Step. The meaning is that to gain control of my own life, I have to let go of the urge—the need—to control the events in my life, and the control of others. The first three steps of the program direct an addict to surrender his control over <u>alcohol</u>; the 13th Step directs a person to surrender his control over his life, after he has learned to control the drug. To do that, I have to "believe" that a power greater than me can "control" people and events according to a plan that I cannot possible conceive of. It sounds contradictory and paradoxical: to be in control, I have to relinquish control.

Who or what can that "power" be, you ask? It can be the God of our fathers, or the religion that you grew up with. Or it can be a group that you belong to, such as the 12 Step self-help groups. Or it can be a belief in Nature, or a Cause to which you dedicate yourself, such as the sanctity of the family. Or it can be a Guru, or an Adult Guarantor, whom you respect as a leader and model.

The point is that to gain serenity, I need to surrender my own ego to a higher power; I cannot be a law unto myself.

Vincent B. Cardarelli, Th.M., CADC

And contrary to what you would expect, if you seek grandeur, if you seek power, status and perfection, you will not achieve serenity.

The chapters in "Toward Serenity" deal with numerous topics in the spirit of the 13th Step. They deal with common sense strategies in various aspects of your life that can help you to attain some measure of serenity. In a sense, this could have been the first chapter in the book, and all the others follow in its spirit. I have chosen to put it last as a summary of all that went before.

I came to believe that my search toward serenity depends upon a constant vigilance against false pride, a constant effort to be humble, and a submission of my will to a power greater than myself.

I wish you Serenity.

Appendix:

The Twelve Steps of the AA Program:
I have often mentioned the 12 Steps in this column; I add them here as a reference for you.

1. We admitted that we were powerless over alcohol—that our lives had become unmanageable.
2. Came to believe that a Power greater than ourselves could restore us to sanity.
3. Made a decision to turn our will and our lives over to the care of God *as we understood Him.*
4. Made a searching and fearless moral inventory of ourselves.
5. Admitted to God, to ourselves, and to another human being the exact nature of our wrongs.
6. Were entirely ready to have God remove all these defects of character.
7. Humbly asked Him to remove our shortcomings.
8. Made a list of all persons we had harmed, and became willing to make amends to them all.
9. Made direct amends to such people whenever possible, except when to do so would injure them or others.
10. Continued to take personal inventory and when we were wrong promptly admitted it.

11. Sought through prayer and meditation to improve our conscious contact with God *as we understood Him,* praying only for knowledge of His will for us and the power to carry that out.
12. Having had a spiritual awakening as the result of these Steps, we tried to carry this message to others, and to practice these principles in all our affairs.

About the Author

Vince Cardarelli lives and works in Clinton, N.J. After retiring from the Catholic Priesthood in 1971, Vince began a career in clinical counseling, working in various settings. His unique contribution has been to combine traditional counseling, the 12 Step Program and spirituality into a unified approach to mental health. He has a Masters in Counseling from Princeton Theological Seminary, and is a New Jersey State Certified Substance Counselor. Besides his clinical practice, he has written for newspapers, lectured extensively on mental health topics and taught in colleges and in a Family Practice Residency Program for 10 years.

Vince is very well-known in the AA and Alanon communities, and excels in marriage counseling for couples who are in recovery.